P.99   (P. 5)
P.124   (P.32)
P.242   P. 57
P.248   P. 62
(P.287) (P. 66)
P.310   (P. 72)
P.350   (P.99)
        P.136
P.139   (P.161)
P.196   (P.199)
(P.207) (P.199)
P.264   (P.310)
(P.323) P. 332
(P.339) (P.364)

2000 *jazz guitar*

Visit us on the Web at http://www.melbay.com — E-mail us at email@melbay.com

Contents

Abercrombie, John 4
   Just in Tune – CD 1, Track 1

Alden, Howard 13
   Thinking of Barney

Baker, Mickey 16
   Blue Jazz Rock – CD 1, Track 2

Barbosa-Lima, Carlos 21
   Embers – CD 1, Track 3

Bay, William 30
   Ee's Flat – CD 1, Track 4
   For Wes – CD 1, Track 5
   Ode for Mr. Van Eps – CD 1, Track 6

Berman, Ron 34
   Esther & Frank – CD 1, Track 7

Bertoncini, Gene 38
   Greensleeves – CD 1, Track 8

Bruno, Jimmy 45
   Eggplant Pizza – CD 1, Track 9

Campbell, Royce 56
   Bb Blues – CD 1, Track 10

Chapman, Charles H. 61
   Harbor Haze – CD 1, Track 11

Christiansen, Corey 65
   Synergy – CD 1, Track 12

Christiansen, Mike 71
   Bonita – CD 1, Track 13

Collins, Cal 76
   Poor Butterfly

de Mause, Alan 81
   The Chameleon – CD 1, Track 14

Diorio, Joe 84
   Reflections of Wes – CD 1, Track 15

Escheté, Ron 90
   Homeward Bound – CD 1, Track 16

Ferguson, Jim 95
   Swing Low Sweet Chariot – CD 1, Track 17

Fite, Buddy 98
   Mr. BeeBop – CD 1, Track 18

Forman, Bruce 106
   Poison Ivy – CD 1, Track 19

Griggs, John 117
   Jive Blues – CD 1, Track 20

Hahn, Jerry 123
   Down To the Wire – CD 1, Track 21

Haydon, Rick .131
   New Folks – CD 1, Track 22

Hendrickson, Al 135
   Jazz Waltz – CD 1, Track 23

Hudson, Roger 138
   Rafaela – CD 1, Track 24

Ingram, Adrian 143
   Dear George – CD 1, Track 25

Jacobs, Sid 149
   Lullaby in Four – CD 1, Track 26

Juber, Laurence 153
   Manhattan Snapshot – CD 1, Track 27

Lawrence, John E. 160
   Home – CD 1, Track 28

Linsky, Jeff 164
   The Love Club – CD 2, Track 1

McCorkle, Dennis 169
   Just for the Thinking – CD 2, Track 2

Mehling, Paul .172
   Swing This – CD 2, Track 3

Contents

Moio, Bill *176*
Time Stood Still – CD 2, Track 4
Flippin' with Bird – CD 2, Track 5

Moretti, Van *191*
Swingin' on 7 – CD 2, Track 6

Morgen, Howard *195*
Ohhh! Susanna – CD 2, Track 7

Muldrow, Ronald *198*
Ra-Fe-El – CD 2, Track 8

Musso, Paul *206*
Moon Flower – CD 2, Track 9

Nichols, Jim *210*
Careless Love – CD 2, Track 10

Petersen, Jack *221*
Groovey! – CD 2, Track 11

Piburn, Bill *227*
Prince John – CD 2, Track 12

Pizzarelli, Bucky *231*
Indy Annie – CD 2, Track 13

Pizzarelli, John *235*
Ep's Frets – CD 2, Track 14

Puma, Joe *241*
BossAngo

Rector, Johnny *247*
Noodlin' at 80 – CD 2, Track 15

Salvador, Sal *252*
Campesina – CD 2, Track 16

Saood, Zafar *256*
Snowforest

Sims, Jerry *263*
Just Like a Dream – CD 2, Track 17

Smith, David *269*
June

Smith, Johnny *275*
Satan's Doll – CD 2, Track 18
Lullaby – CD 2, Track 19

Sokolow, Fred *286*
Baby Brother – CD 2, Track 20

Solow, Stanley *292*
Opus Untitled – CD 2, Track 21

Standring, Chris *296*
First of December – CD 2, Track 22

Stewart, Jimmy *301*
Autumn Nocturne – CD 2, Track 23

Summers, Andy *304*
Evans Above – CD 2, Track 24

Taylor, Martin *309*
Anything Goes – CD 3, Track 1

Umble, Jay *317*
Groovin' at Nick's – CD 3, Track 2

Upchurch, Phil *322*
Wes's Groove – CD 3, Track 3

Van Eps, George *327*
Midnight
Squattin' at the Grotto – CD 3, Track 4

Viola, Al *336*
Sostenuto – CD 3, Track 5

Wilkins, Jack *338*
For Baden – CD 3, Track 6

Wohlrab, Stephen *349*
Pair of Fives – CD 3, Track 7

Wyble, Jimmy *357*
Two Moods (For Lily)

Zaradin, John *363*
Faivo Klokti – CD 3, Track 8

John Abercrombie

Born in 1944, Port Chester, New York, John Abercrombie grew up in Greenwich, Connecticut, and began playing the guitar at fourteen years of age. By the time he was out of high school, he was ready to veer away from imitative Chuck Berry licks in favor of learning to play the instrument more seriously. While enrolled at Boston's Berklee School of Music, Abercrombie worked with other students and played local clubs and bars. "It was pretty much your standard guitar-organ-drums set up."

An offer to tour with organist Johnny Hammond Smith led to his going to the road for weeks at a time, playing such spots as Count Basie's Lounge and the Club Baron in Harlem. During that same period, Abercrombie met the Brecker Brothers who were in the process of forming Dreams. They invited Abercrombie to play with them, and he was heard on Dreams' debut album on Columbia.

In 1969, following graduation, Abercrombie decided to head South in hopes of breaking into the New York music scene. In the next few years he developed into one of New York's most in-demand session musicians. He did record dates with Gil Evans, Gato Barbieri, Barry Miles and many other artists, and also became a regular with Chico Hamilton's group.

It was as the guitarist in Billy Cobham's band that Abercrombie first began attracting widespread attention among the general public. This ensemble was something of a Dreams reunion since it also included the Brecker Brothers. Abercrombie is heard on Cobham's *Crosswinds*, *Total Eclipse* and on *Current Events*, released in 1988, John used guitar synthesizer for the first time on record. *John Abercrombie/Marc Johnson/Peter Erskine*, released in 1989, was recorded in Boston on April 21, 1988 and documents this innovative trio live. Repertoire from their four-year association is presented, and standards often linked with Bill Evans are given resplendent treatment.

John's affinity for jazz standards complements his role as an active clinician and teacher. In listening-preparation for a Harvard lecture, where John surveyed the history of jazz guitar, he explained: "When I'm playing tunes like *Autumn Leaves* or *Stella By Starlight*, as much as I've played those tunes over the years, I still enjoy playing them. And because I know them so well, I'm very free with them. I'm just as free with them as when I'm playing with no chords at all. That, to me, is free jazz."

John Abercrombie possesses a unique voice as a jazz guitarist combining evolving technologies with a tradition well-represented by jazz standards. Further insight into music comes forth in a 1988 *Jazziz* interview: "Carrying the tradition of jazz guitar from Charlie Christian and Django Reinhardt to the present day is a very important aspect of my music...I'd like people to perceive me as having a direct connection to the history of jazz guitar, while expanding some musical boundaries which may not always involve the guitar itself." On the 1990 release *Animato*, John collaborates with composer/synthesist Vince Mendoza and drummer Jon Christensen and presents eight original compositions.

CD #1
Track #1

Just In Tune

John Abercrombie

Guitar Intro

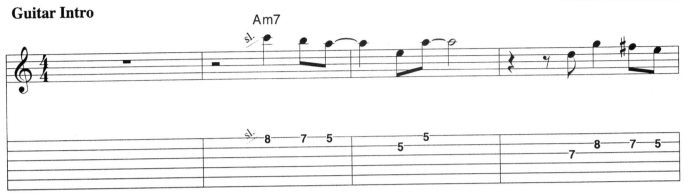

Used by Permission

Trumpet plays melody with rhythmic liberties on recording

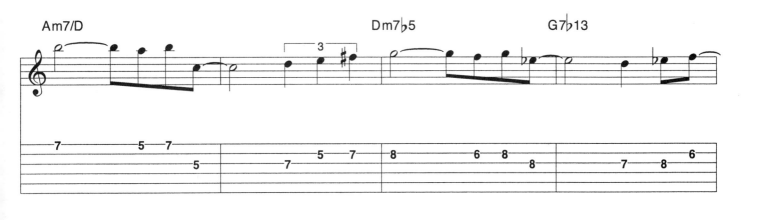

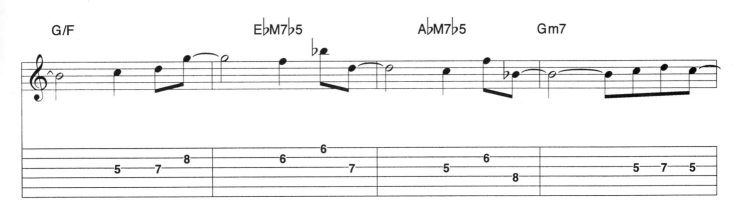

To Coda ⊕ last time.

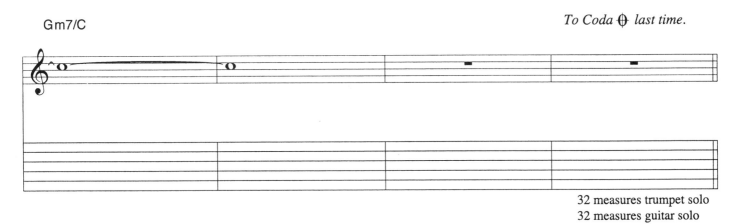

32 measures trumpet solo
32 measures guitar solo
32 measures organ solo

7

Guitar Solo

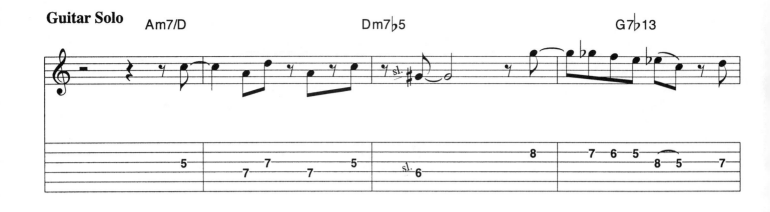

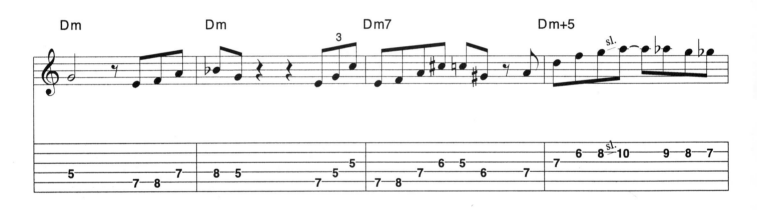

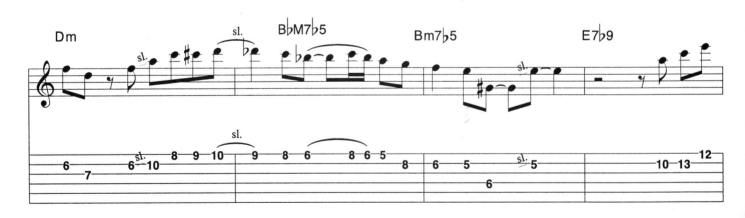

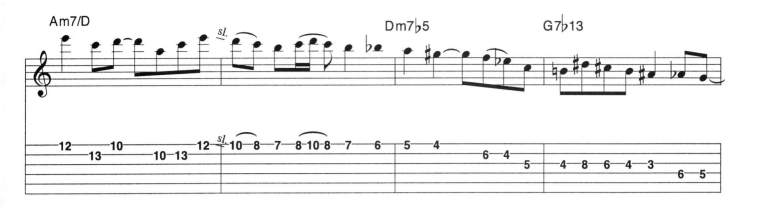

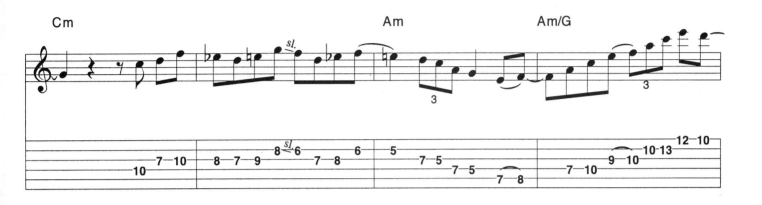

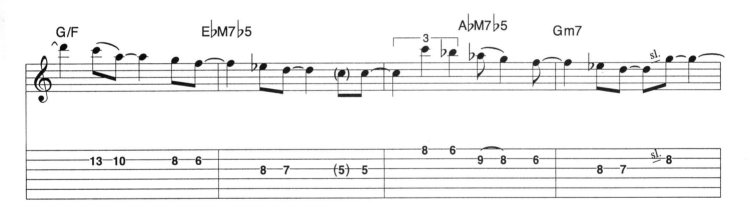

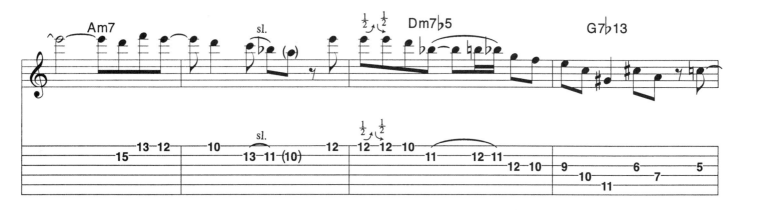

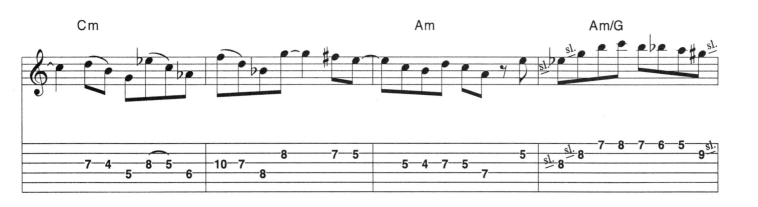

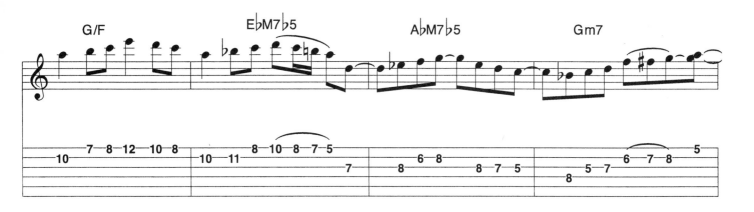

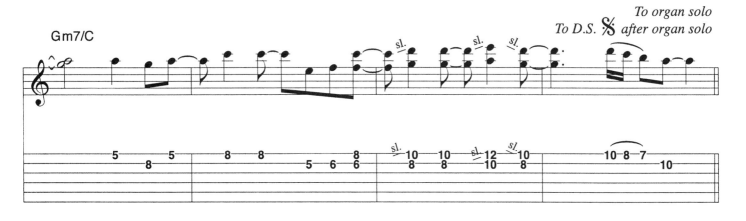

11

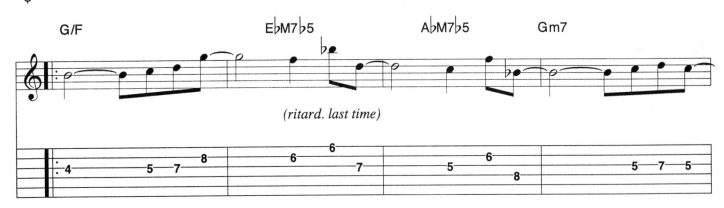

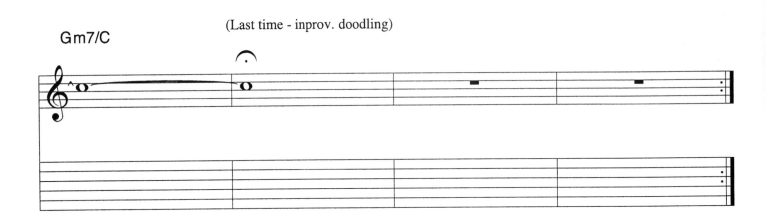

Howard Alden

Born in Newport Beach, California, in 1958, Howard Alden began playing at age ten, inspired by recordings of Armstrong, Basie and Goodman, as well as those by guitarists Barney Kessel, Charlie Christian, Django Reinhardt and George Van Eps. Soon he was working professionally around Los Angeles playing in groups ranging from traditional to mainstream to modern jazz. In 1979, Alden went east, for a summer in Atlantic City with Red Norvo, and continued to perform with him frequently for several years.

Upon Moving to New York City in 1982, Alden's skills, both as soloist and accompanist, were quickly recognized and sought-out for appearances and recordings with such artists as Joe Bushkin, Ruby Braff, Joe Williams, Warren Varché and Woody Herman. He has continued to win accolades from critics and musicians alike, adding Benny Carter, Flip Phillips, Mel Powell, Bud Freeman, Kenny Davern, Clark Terry, Dizzy Gillespie and George Van Eps, as well as notable contemporaries such as Scott Hamilton and Ken Peplowski to his list of impressive credits.

Howard Alden has been a Concord Jazz recording artist since the late '80s where his prolific recorded output as leader, co-leader, and versatile sideman, has captured an artist of consistently astonishing virtuosity and originality. One of the many highlights in Howard Alden's fruitful association with Concord Jazz came in 1991 when, at the urging of Concord President, Carl Jefferson, Alden recorded with one of his all-time heroes, seven-string guitar master George Van Eps on the album *Thirteen Strings* (CCD-4464).

As a result of his association with - and inspiration from - George Van Eps, Alden has been playing the seven-string guitar exclusively since 1992. The seven string guitar imparts a greater range and harmonic richness to Alden's already colorful tonal palette, as evidenced on the three remarkable follow-up albums with Van Eps, his critically acclaimed duo recordings with saxophonist/clarinetist Ken Peplowski, and the stunning interplay between Alden and special guest Frank Wess on *Your Story - The Music of Bill Evans* (CCD4621). Alden also teamed up with fellow guitarists Jimmy Bruno and Frank Vignola to record a three guitar outing entitled *The Concord Jazz Guitar Collective* (CCD-4672), which was quickly called by some critics "an instant classic!"

Thinking of Barney

Howard Alden

Mickey Baker

Mickey Baker's reputation amongst many guitarists is mainly as an author of various guitar books and tutors. But he has also been a professional guitarist mainly in the field of rhythm and blues music. He is still musically active but now lives in Paris with his wife Sylvia.

As a boy Baker lived in an orphanage and it was in this institution's marching band that he first developed an interest in music. At the age of sixteen he ran away from the orphanage and ended up in New York paying his way as a laborer. By the time he was nineteen, having listened to many leading jazz musicians, including Charlie Parker and Dizzy Gillespie, Baker decided that he wanted to be a jazz musician. The trumpet was his first choice but the finance needed to purchase this instrument was too high, so at the age of nineteen he decided to buy a guitar.

After a few years study, including a short spell at the New York School of Music, Mickey Baker developed the ability, in 1949, to form his own jazz group. This venture was not a financial success so he decided to move to California. There the reception to his progressive style of jazz music was even less successful. While he was trying to earn the money needed to get back to New York, Baker heard blues guitarist, Pee Wee Creighton. He liked what he heard and saw that Creighton was earning a good living. The result was that Baker changed his guitar style and returned to New York as a blues guitarist. His decision proved correct as Mickey Baker, blues guitarist, found himself much in demand for the Atlantic, Savoy and King labels as a backing artist for top blues artists, including Ray Charles, Big Joe Turner, Ruth Brown, and The Drifters.

During the mid 1950s Baker felt he could improve his financial status by emulating the chart topping duo of guitar wizard Les Paul and singer Mary Ford. He joined forces with an ex-student of his named Sylvia and in 1957 they had a smash hit with a song called *Love is Strange*. Their popularity was to last right through to 1961. With this success behind them the Bakers were financially able to establish their own publishing and recording companies, as well as their own nightclub.

Since the early 1950s Mickey Baker had been working on his tutors and music albums and through his own publishing company, he was able to achieve worldwide distribution for these works.

Despite his success as a blues and popular guitarist Baker felt that he still wished to play jazz guitar again. He therefore decided to move with his wife to Europe where he hoped he could develop a more fulfilling musical life.

He bought a home in Paris and established permanent French residency there. Since that time Mickey Baker has prospered writing, arranging, leading various groups and has to a great extent fulfilled his desire to continue playing his own distinctive style of jazz and blues guitar.

Blue Jazz Rock

Mickey Baker

Swing

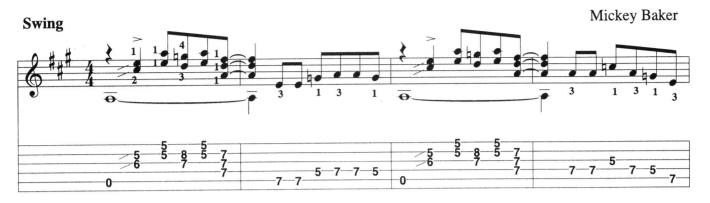

© Mickey Baker

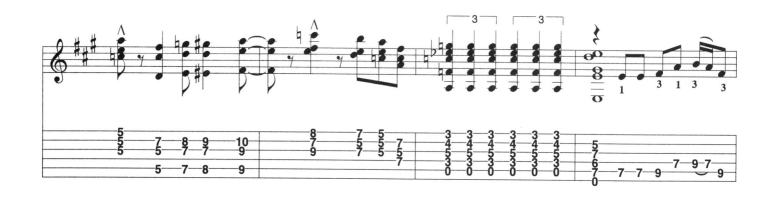

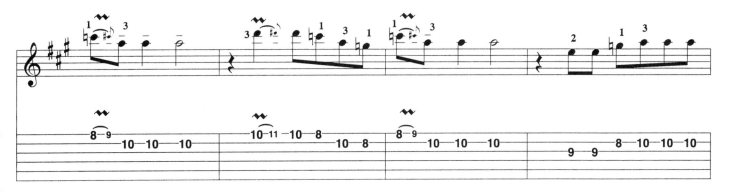

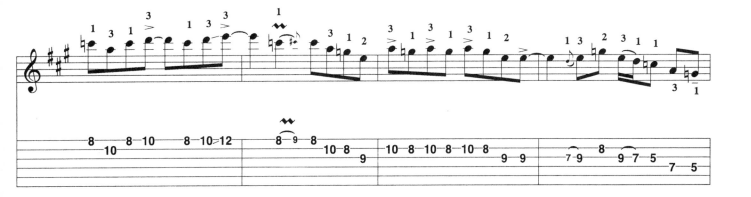

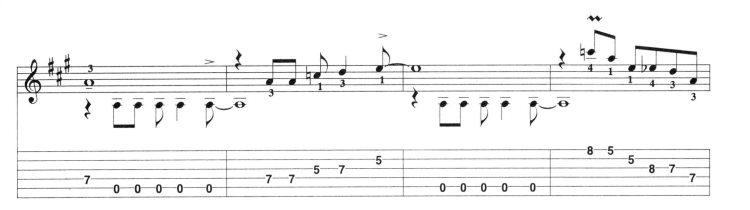

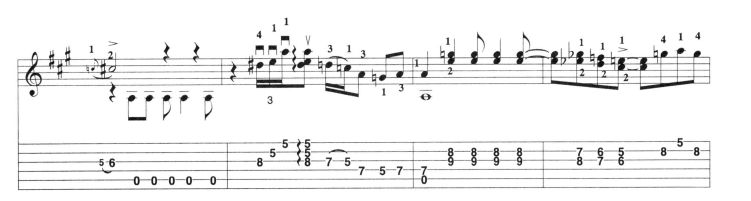

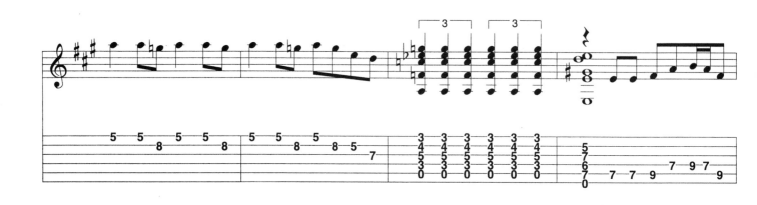

Carlos Barbosa-Lima

Born in 1944 in São Paulo, Brazil, Carlos Barbosa-Lima began studying the guitar at the age of seven, making his concert debut five years later in São Paulo and Rio de Janeiro. Since his United States debut in 1967, Mr. Barbosa-Lima has enjoyed a global concert career marked by numerous distinguished recordings. The breadth of his repertoire and his unique ability to integrate diverse musical styles are strong features of his work.

Embers

by John Griggs
Carlos Barbosa-Lima

Introd.
Lento (Rubato) (with a certain feeling of movement)

(bass wthout pizz. but always keeping a muted quality)

23

IMPROVISATION

*Light *pizz.* (thumb plucks with flesh): upper voice chords played very *staccato* with *i-m-a* brushing respective strings rapidly and in parallel position to the strings — producing a percussive effect in off-beat.

Embers

by John Griggs
Carlos Barbosa-Lima

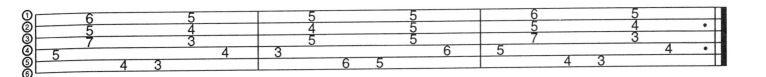

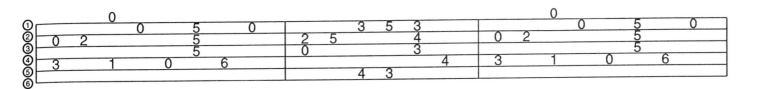

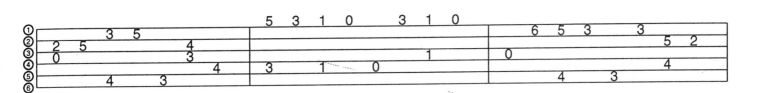

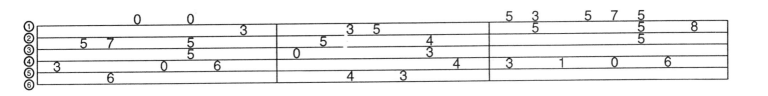

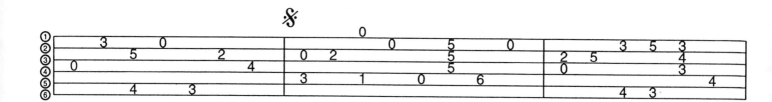

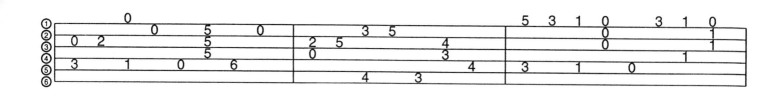

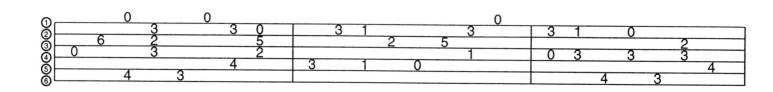

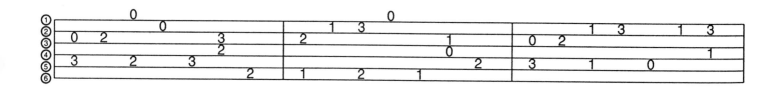

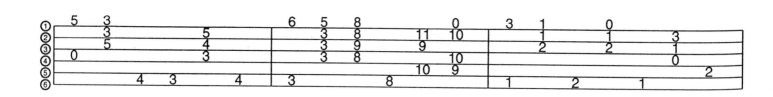

Improvisation

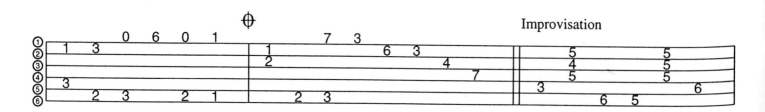

28

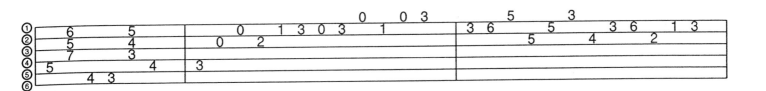

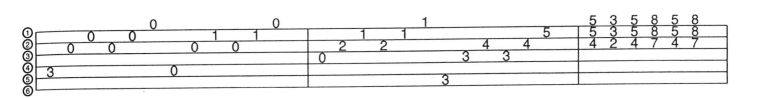

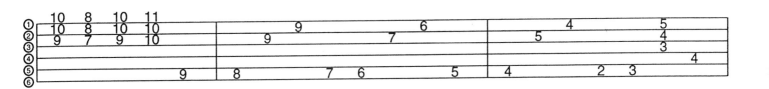

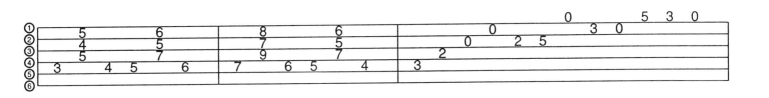

Dal $ al $\oplus$ e Fine

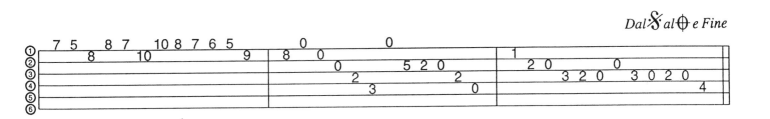

Fine

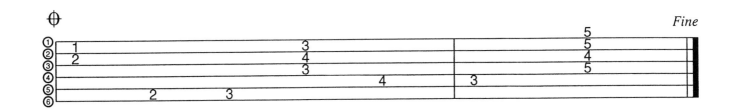

William Bay

William Bay is president of Mel Bay Publications, Inc. He began playing the trumpet at the age of 5 and became an accomplished soloist featured with bands and orchestras throughout the St. Louis area. For years, he led his own jazz orchestra. Bill is also a fine guitarist who has performed in a wide variety of professional musical settings. He received his undergraduate degree from Washington University in St. Louis and his master's degree from the University of Missouri/Columbia. Bill has written over 100 books dealing with a wide assortment of musical topics, instruments, and proficiency levels, with sales in the millions.

Ee's Flat

William Bay

Jazz Feeling ♩ = *130*

Fine

D.C. al Fine

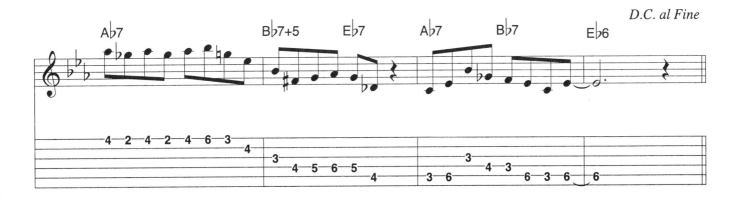

31

For Wes

Moderately, Jazz Feeling ♩ = *144*

William Bay

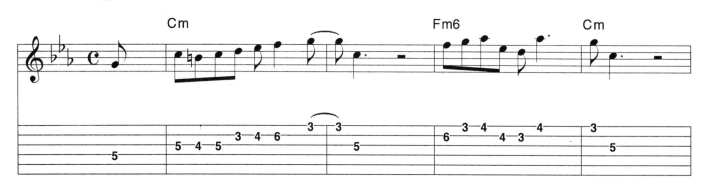

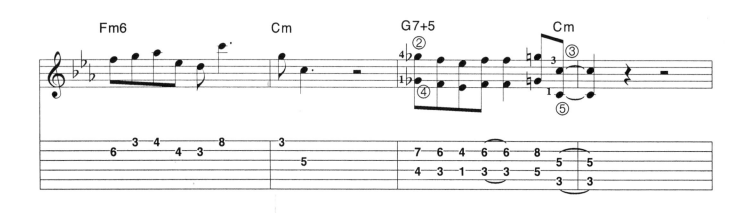

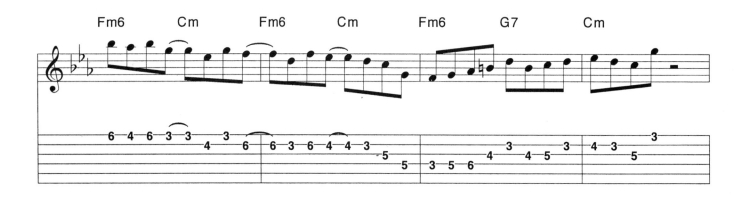

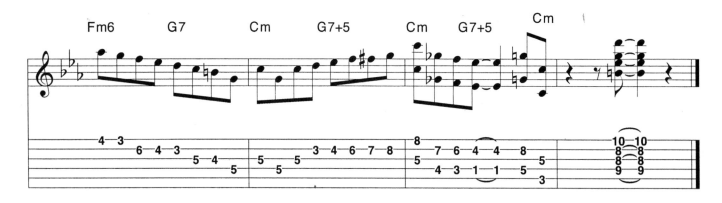

Ode For Mr. Van Eps

William Bay

Fingerstyle
Slow swing

♩ = 112

Fine

D.C. al Fine

Ron Berman

Ron has studied classical guitar with Chris Boydston and John Jervis, jazz guitar with Mick Goodrick and Chuck Wayne, composition with George Russell and arranging and orchestration with Jaki Byard and Phil Wilson. He received a Masters Degree in Composition from the New England Conservatory in 1978. Since moving to Los Angeles in 1981, in addition to performing, Ron has written and recorded music for film and television and teaches part-time at Pasadena City College and Harbor College. His fingerstyle chord, linear and rhythmic approach has broadened the spectrum of Jazz Guitar. You can hear Ron on the CD *Swing Team* released in 1998 (ASTRON Records).

Esther & Frank

arranged for solo guitar by Ron Berman

Ron Berman

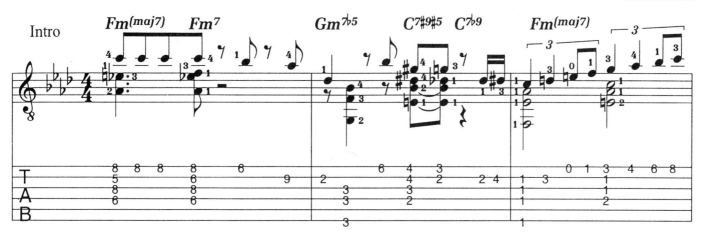

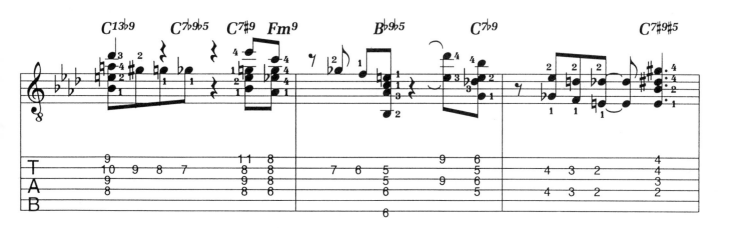

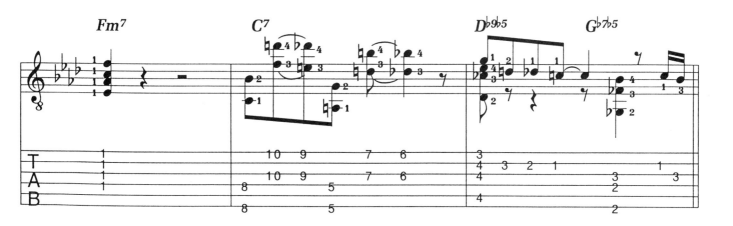

35

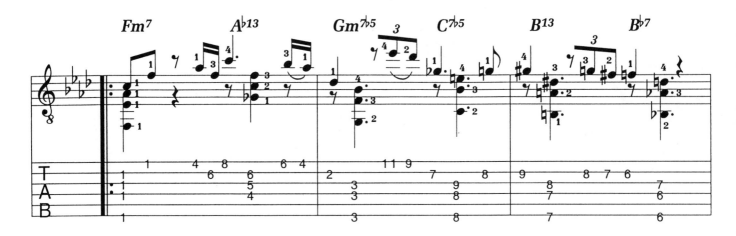

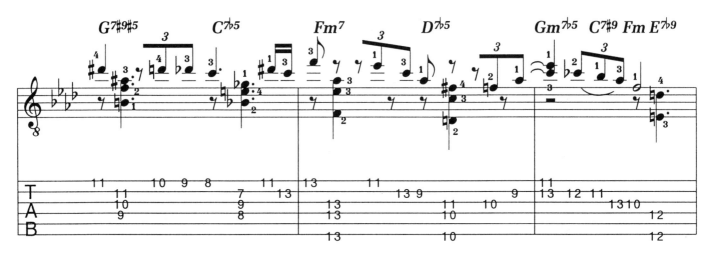

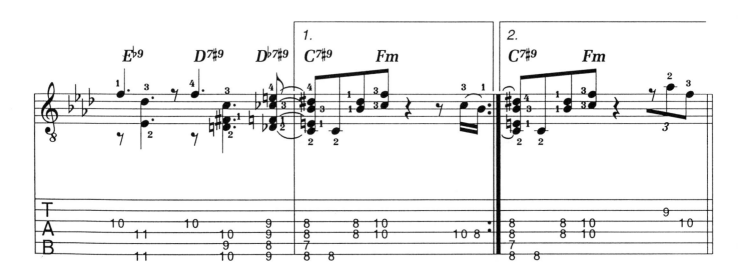

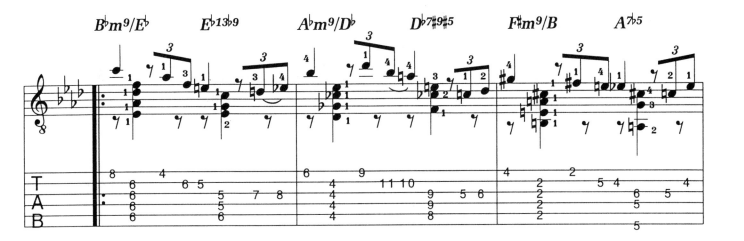

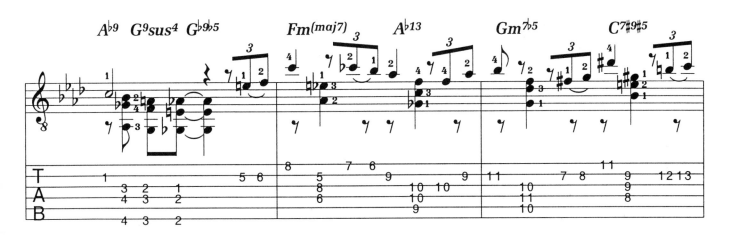

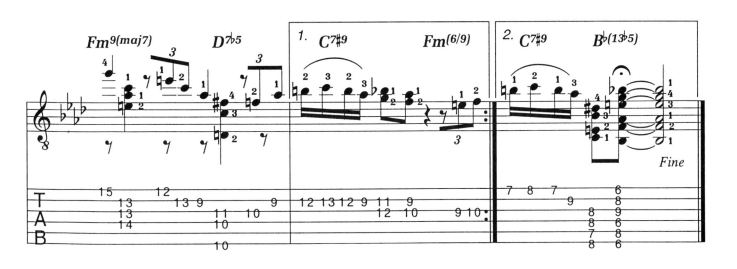

Gene Bertoncini

Gene Bertoncini has firmly established himself as one of the most eloquent and versatile masters of the guitar. With elegance and ease, he bridges the jazz, classical, pop, and bossa nova styles, integrating his own spontaneous and tasteful improvisations along the way. He has earned highest critical regard for his artistry on both the classical and electric guitar.

Bertoncini has worked with the Metropolitan Opera orchestra, the Benny Goodman Sextet; singers Tony Bennett, Morgana King, Lena Horne, Vic Damone and Edye Gorme; jazzmen Buddy Rich, Wayne Shorter, Hubert Laws, Clark Terry, Paul Desmond, and Paul Winter; and arranger/composers Lalo Schifrin and Michel LeGrand, among others. He has performed regularly on the Merv Griffin and Johnny Carson shows, and has been one of the most prolific and popular studio musicans in New York City. For the past eight years Bertoncini has performed with bassist Michael Moore in a duo which *The New York Times* describes as "...one of the finest pairings of jazz strings..."

Bertoncini's teaching credits include the Eastman School of Music where he regularly performs and conducts summer workshops for jazz guitarists, the New England Conservatory, New York University, and the Banff School of Fine Arts. He has been a highly sought-after guest clinician in colleges and universities throughout the country.

Greensleeves

Arr. Gene Bertoncini

D = IMPROVISED SECTION

42

43

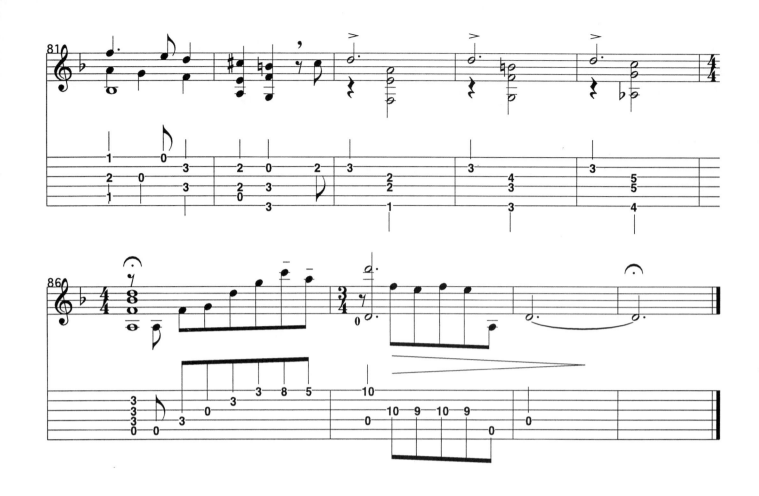

Jimmy Bruno

Jazz musicians are very special breed. With their music they tell of a world unknown to most, a world where mediocrity is nonexistent and the pursuit of perfection prevails. The wonderful art of jazz is a medium whereby the musician is given the freedom to flee from an otherwise ordinary dimension and share with us his insights, dreams and artistic passion.

Since the beginning of time there have been those who stood out from the crowd—those who did something different, something special. Something nobody else thought of doing, nor was able to do. Obviously, I speak of Jimmy Bruno. When Jimmy performs, he explodes with a rare determination and burning desire to show the listener his world. Jimmy is a gift to us. Listening to him play is an inspiration.

—Bob Benedetto, November 1998

****

In 1998 during the celebration of the 100th anniversary of the archtop guitar Jimmy bruno was honored with a special concert at the Smithsonian Institution recognizing him as one of the true masters of guitar and one of the preeminent jazz musicians of his generation. From the perspective of the Smithsonian, Jimmy Bruno's artistry exemplifies the spirit of musical refinement and innovation that has made the archtop guitar the quintessential American musical instrument. In addition to his own fine albums, Jimmy has played and recorded with the most distinguished artists in jazz. He is held in the highest esteem by both critics and fellow musicians and is regarded as one of the most important guitarists to appear on the jazz scene in many years. In technical terms, he has taken the very difficult 7-string guitar to a new level of harmonic invention. His approach has already been felt in both the professional and academic musical communities with countless guitarists copying and analyzing what is now appreciated as the "Jimmy bruno style of guitar playing." Jimmy Bruno is, indeed, in the process the of revolutionizing jazz guitar. That he should be doing so at a comparatively young age for jazz musicians is all the more testament to his talent.

—Randall Kremer, Smithsonian Institution

Egg Plant Pizza

This tune came about when I was playing at J.J.'s Grotto, a small jazz club in Philly that featured great pizza. Eggplant pizza was one of their specialties. When the place would get overcrowded one of the owners would run up to the band stand and tell the band to take a break. I never knew what to play when this happened so I just starting playing blues in B♭. After awhile this little theme emerged.

It is a simple twelve bar blues that is based primarily on a B♭ blues scale. On beats 3 and 4 of bar 8, I depart from the scale with a B6 arpeggio with a ♯5. I was really hearing a G7-9+5. The phrase continues with typical be-bop lines. Some interesting measures to check out are measures 31 and 32. I superimposed different arpeggios over the traditional changes. Measure 42 was a surprise even to me. It's a funny thing when I am playing over tunes I don't preconceive any devices; I just use my ear and try to play what I hear in my head. When I saw this measure written out I was taken aback. I tried to play this measure again and I must confess that I could not play thirteen notes over four beats. Check out the grace note. I found this very amusing but impossible to play. Such is the nature of jazz.

Eggplant Pizza

Introduction

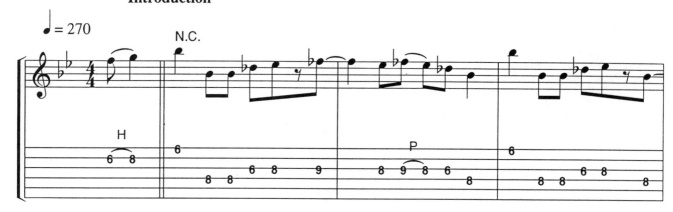

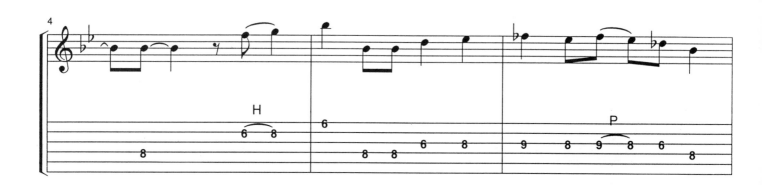

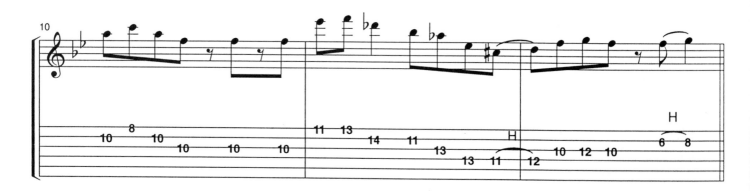

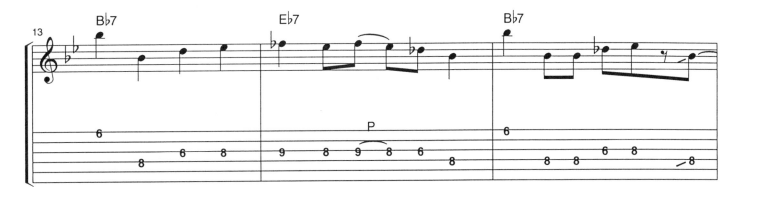

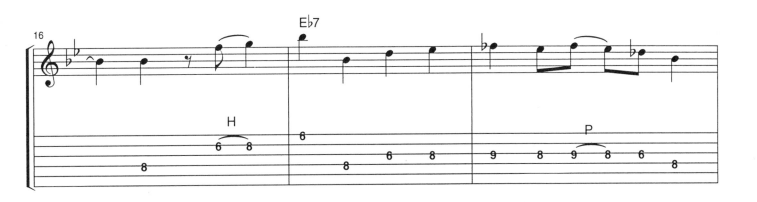

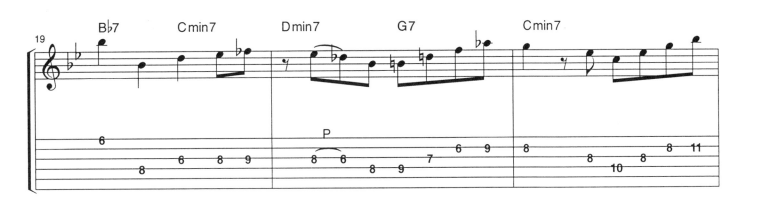

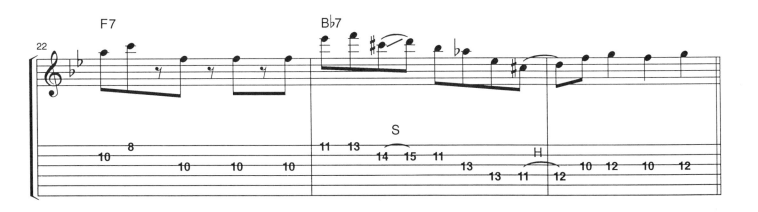

Guitar Solo (1st 7 choruses)

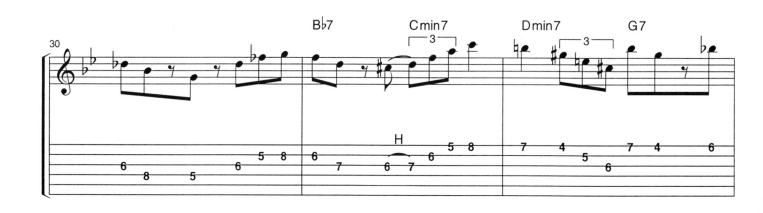

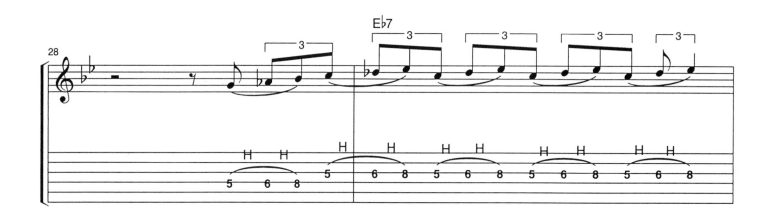

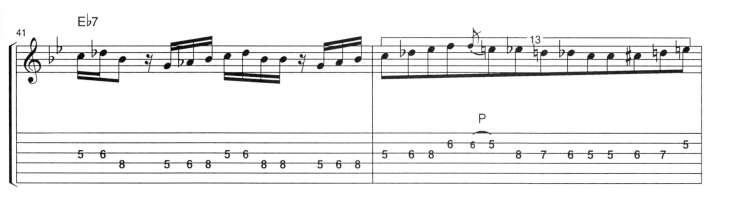

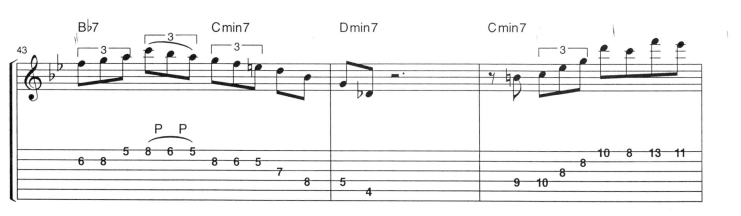

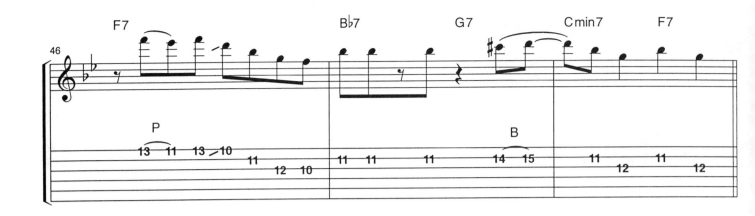

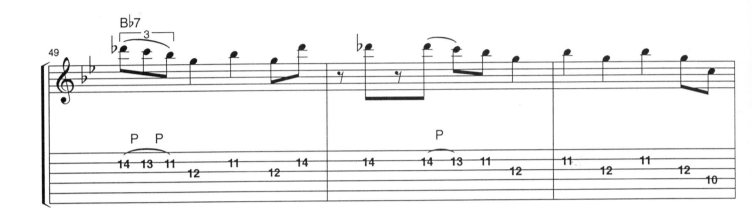

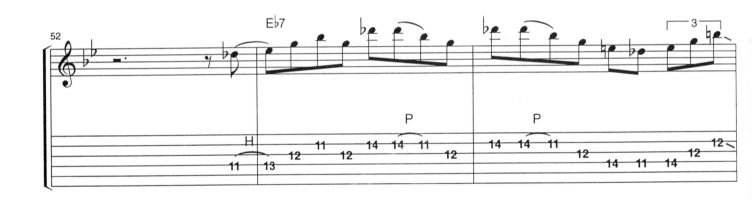

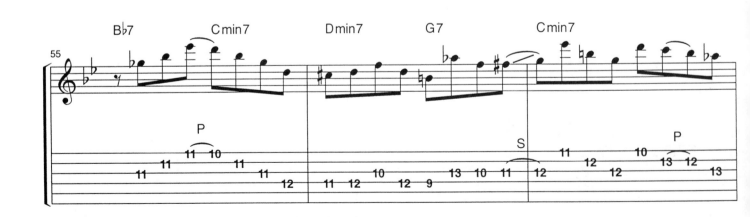

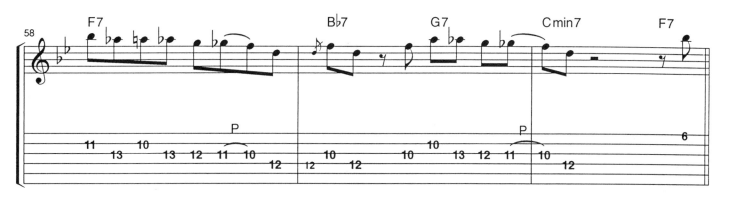

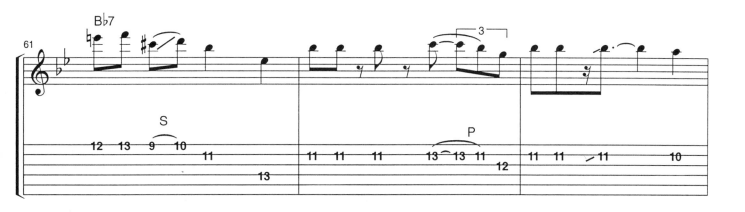

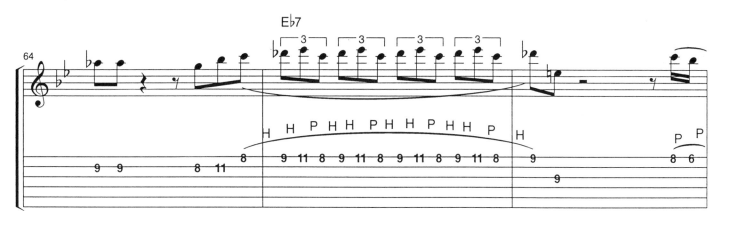

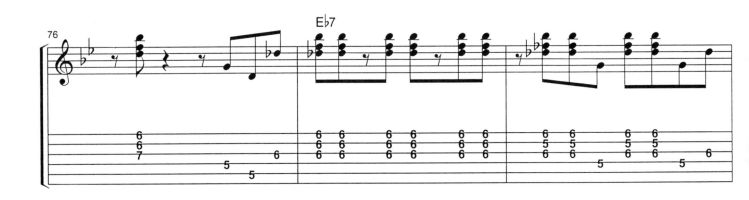

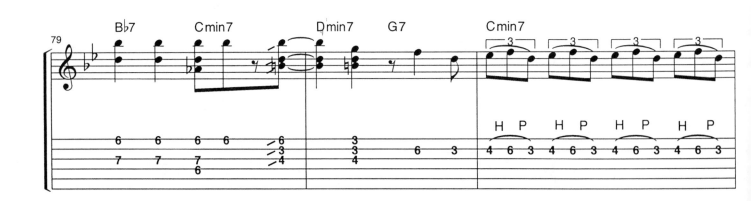

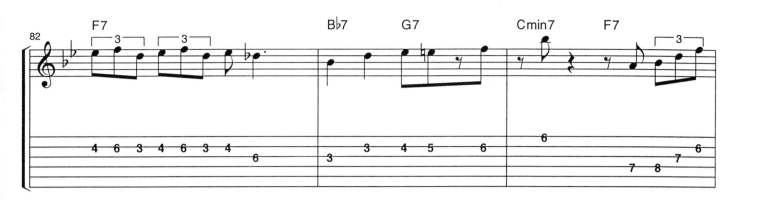

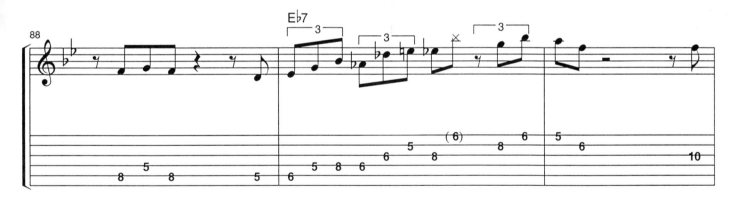

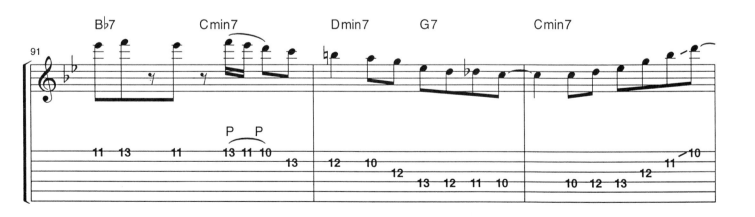

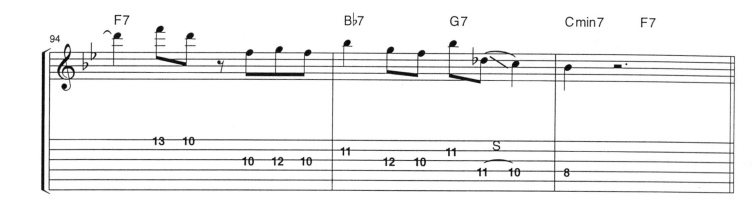

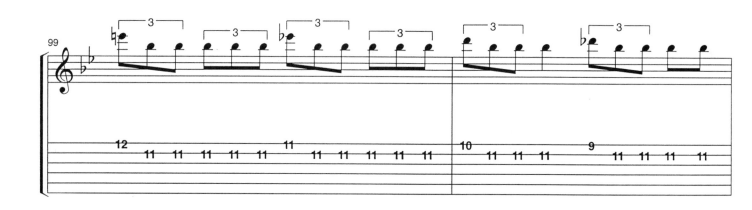

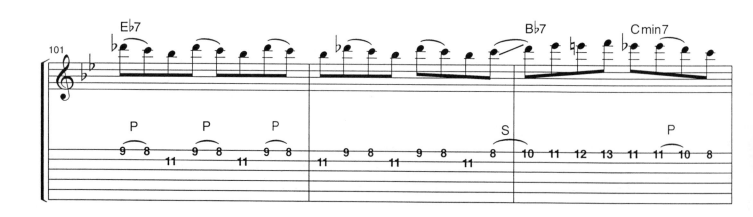

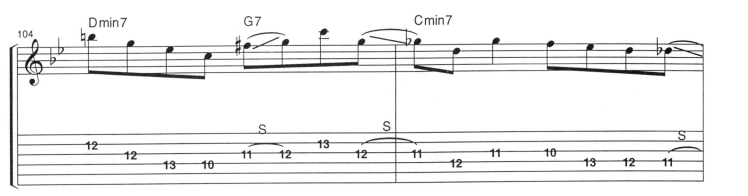

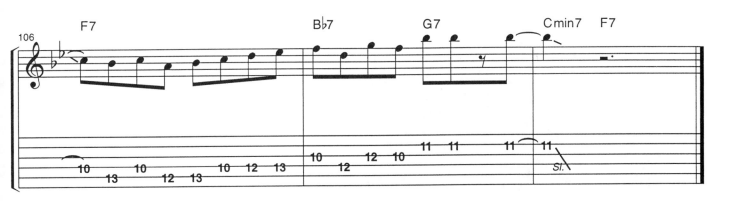

Royce Campbell

Photo by Larry Goshen

Royce Cambell has had a diverse career performing in jazz venues, with symphony orchestras and with Broadway musicals. He has toured with Marvin Gaye, Mel Torme, Perry Como, Cleo Laine and was the guitarist for Henry Mancini for nineteen years until Mancini's death in 1994.

Campbell has released twelve CDs, either as leader or co-leader, and has appeared as a sideman on over thirty recordings. He has recorded with some of the most legendary guitarists in jazz including Pat Martino, Jimmy Raney, John Abercrombie, Tal Farlow, Bucky Pizzarelli, Charlie Byrd, Mundell Lowe, Gene Bertoncini, John Pisano, Larry Coryell, Cal Collins, and Herb Ellis. Campbell produced and performed on the successful CD, *Project G-5, A Tribute to Wes Montgomery* (Episode), which included Herb Ellis, Cal Collins, Tal Farlow, and Jimmy Raney. Campbell cites Wes Montgomery as his primary influence.

Bb Blues

Royce Campbell

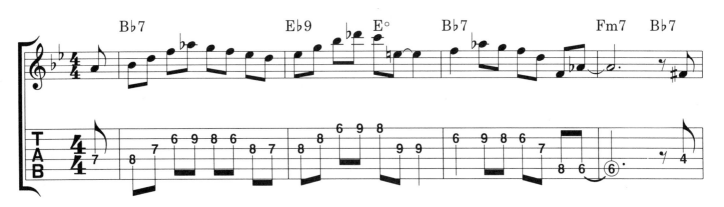

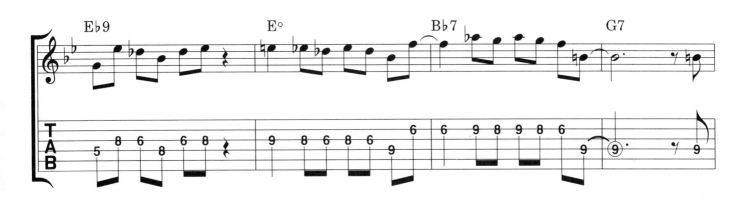

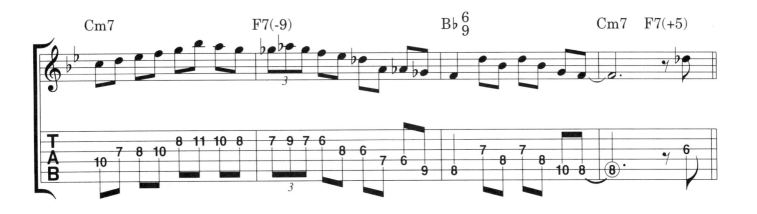

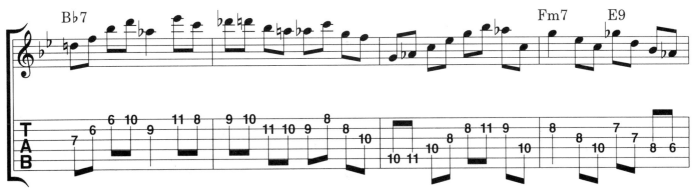

Used by Permission

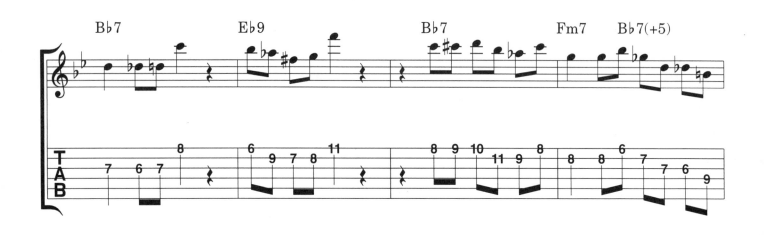

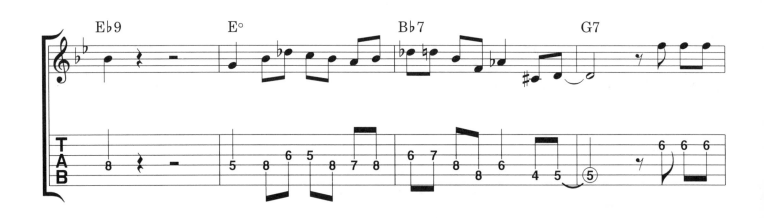

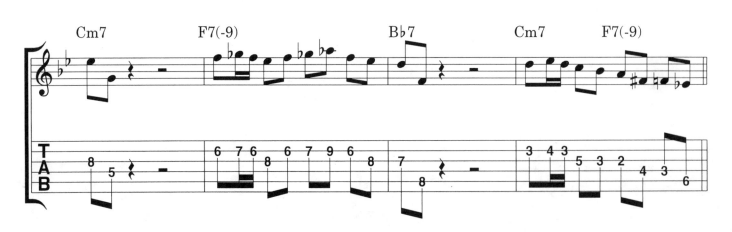

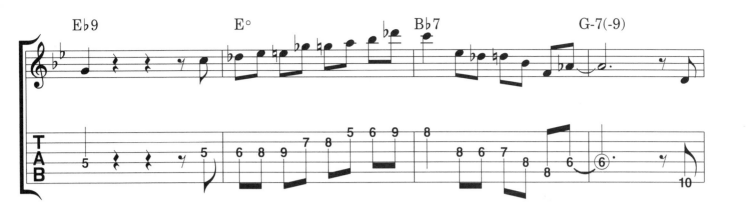

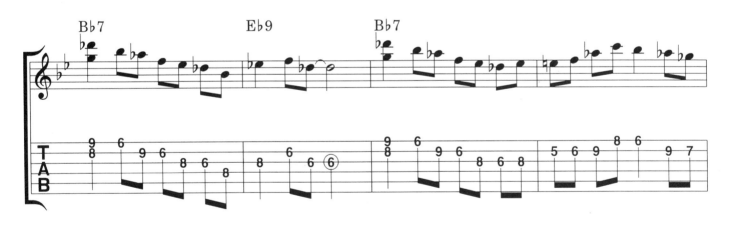

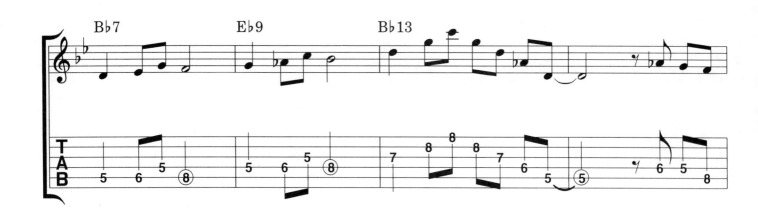

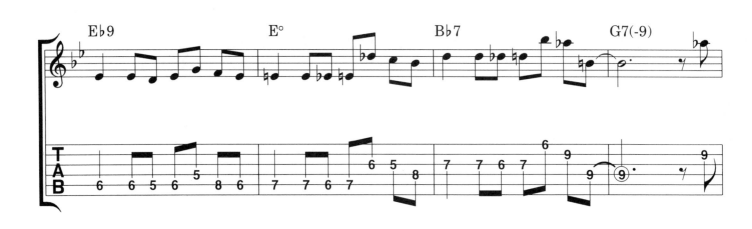

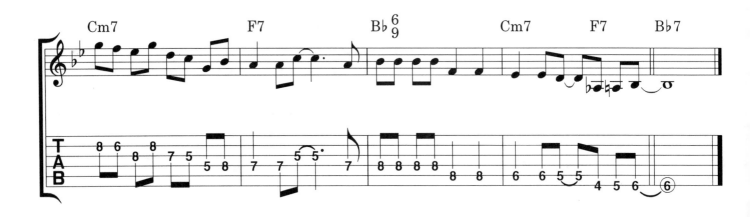

Charles H. Chapman

Charles H. Chapman is a Professor in the Guitar Department at Berklee College of Music where he has taught since 1972. He is a versatile jazz guitarist with extensive performing and recording experience. Charles has appeared in the "pit bands" of such notable theater productions as: *Grease, Will Rogers Follies, Man of La Mancha, Annie, Finian's Rainbow, Fiddler On The Roof, Mame* and *Anything Goes*. He released a jazz duet album with bassist Rich Appleman in 1996, *In Black and White* on DC Records. Since 1997 he has performed at the California NAMM Show; featured with legendary bassist Jerry Jemmott at the 1998 New York Guitar Show as well as a featured performer at the "George Van Eps Tribute Concert" during the "1999 L.A. Jazz Guitar Festival." Charles now performs on a regular basis at guitar shows and jazz festivals internationally.

As a music journalist he has interviewed many of the most prominent guitarists in the field and is a frequent contributor to *Guitar Player, Guitar Shop, Acoustic Guitar, Guild Gallery* and *Just Jazz Guitar* magazines.

As a music copyist Charles has worked for such prestigious publishing houses as Mel Bay, Schirmer, Hal Leonard, Berklee Press and numerous music periodicals, as well as many prominent arrangers.

Charles is an Artist Endorser for *Fender/Guild Corporation* and *Double Treble* custom guitar straps.

Harbor Haze

Comp. & arr. by C. Chapman

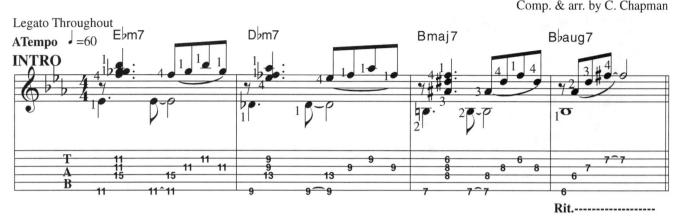
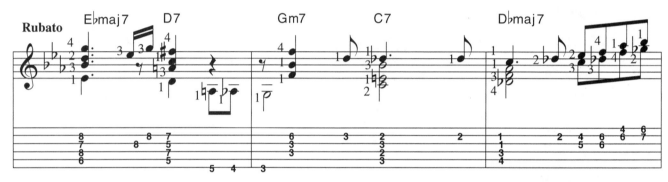
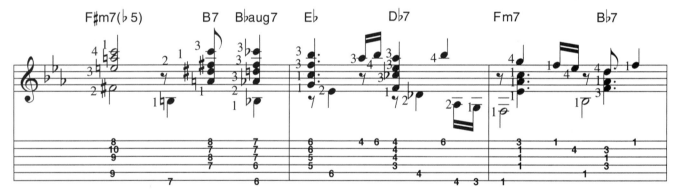
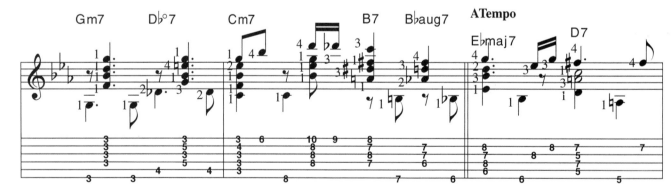

Used by Permission

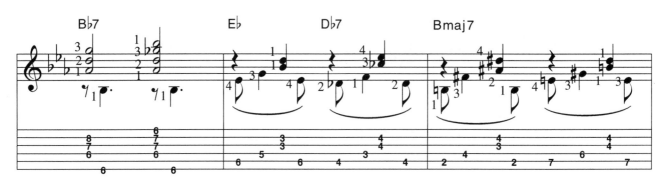

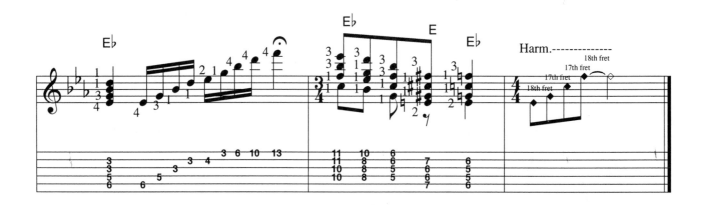

Corey Christiansen

Corey Christiansen was introduced to the guitar at the age of five by his father Mike Christiansen. After receiving a bachelors degree in guitar performance from Utah State University, his education continued with graduate studies with legendary jazz guitar educator Jack Petersen at the University of South Florida, and is now their adjunct faculty guitar teacher. Corey was given the outstanding jazz guitarist award at the Lionel Hampton Jazz Festival in 1995 and 1996. Corey performs regularly in Florida, has released a jazz guitar duo CD entitled *Synergy*, and teaches class as a graduate teaching assistant at the University of South Florida.

Synergy

Corey Christiansen

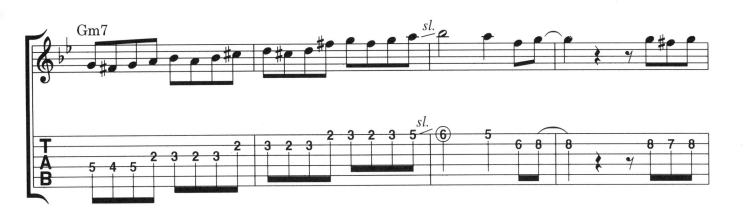

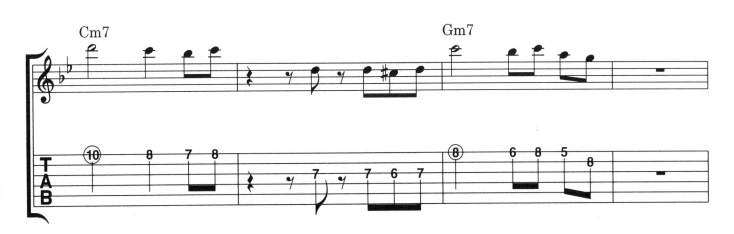

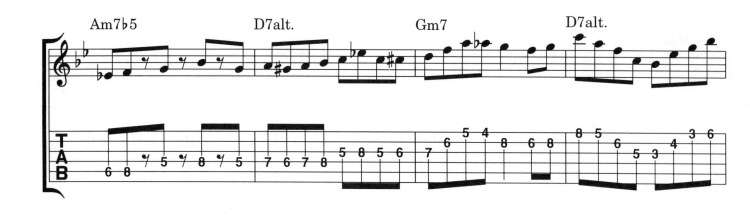

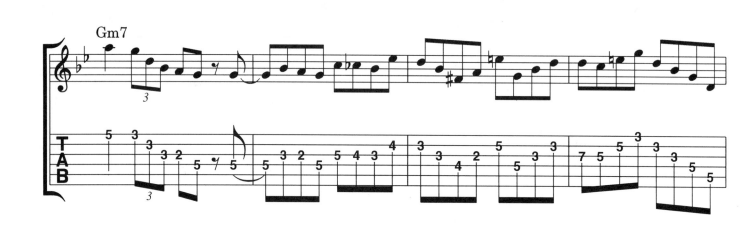

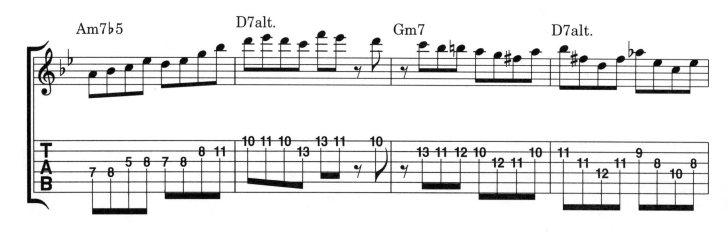

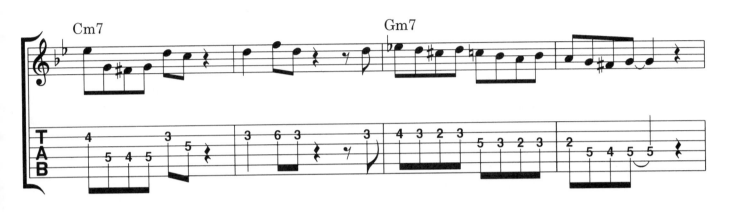

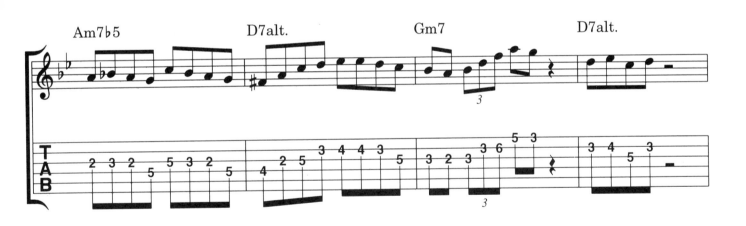

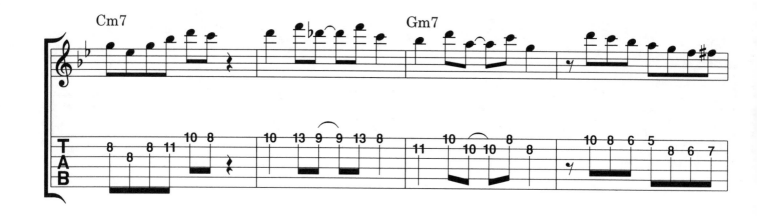

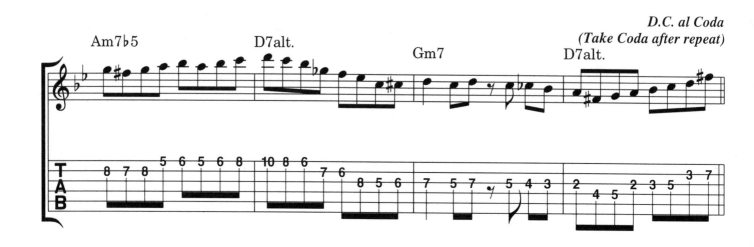

D.C. al Coda
(Take Coda after repeat)

Mike Christiansen

Mike Christiansen is a Professor and Director of Guitar Studies in the Music Department at Utah State University where he was presented with the 1994 Professor of the Year Award. He has conducted many workshops for guitarists and educators. Mike has played in various ensembles and bands, has written and recorded radio jingles, done back-up work on recordings, and has written and recorded for TV and educational films. In addition to performing as a soloist, Mike is a member of the groups Mirage and The Lightwood Duo.

Bonita
(for Kathy)

Mike Christiansen

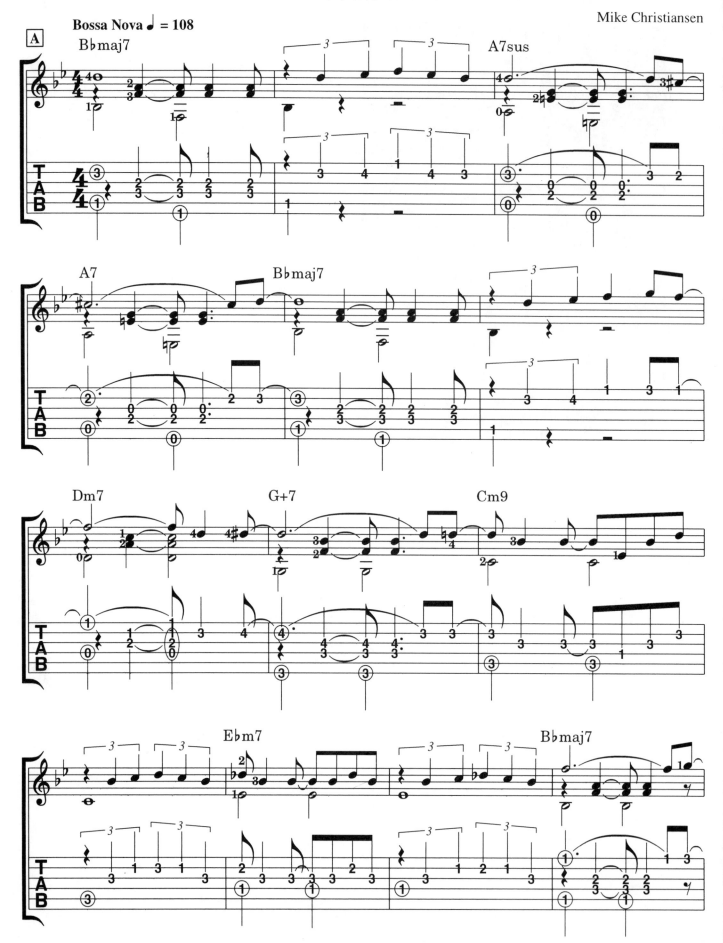

Used by Permission

* Section B is an improvisation over the chord changes of section A.

Cal Collins

Cal Collins was born in Indiana and was influenced by a number of pianists including Art Tatum, Fats Waller, George Shearing and Nat "King" Cole. In the 1950s he moved to Cincinnati and later joined up with the Benny Goodman band.

Carl Jefferson, after hearing Cal play at the Concord Jazz Festival, signed him up as the Concord Records staff guitarist. Cal Collins subsequently played and toured with many of the big names in jazz and in the music business including Herb Ellis, Scott Hamilton, Buddy Tate, Al Cohn, Rosemary Clooney and Terry Gibbs.

Poor Butterfly

Cal Collins

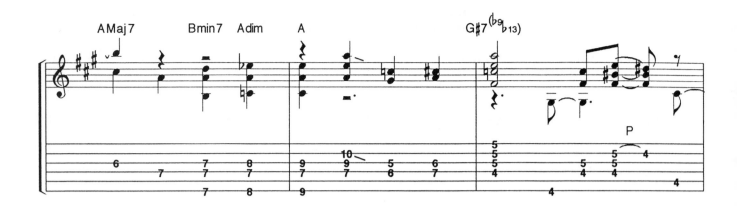

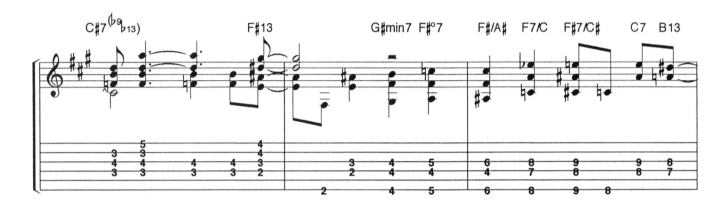

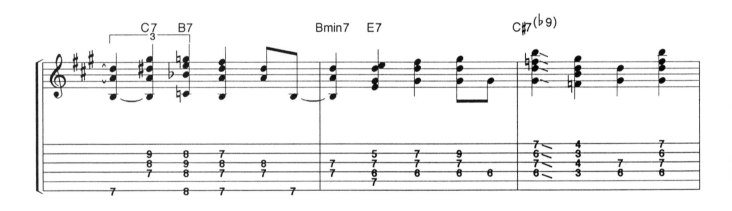

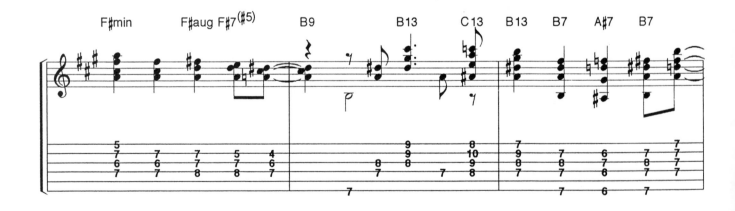

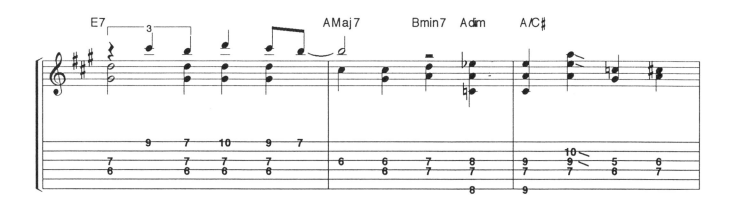

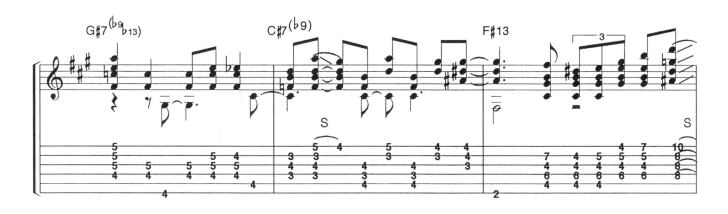

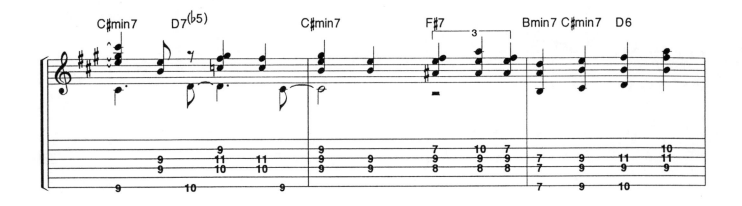

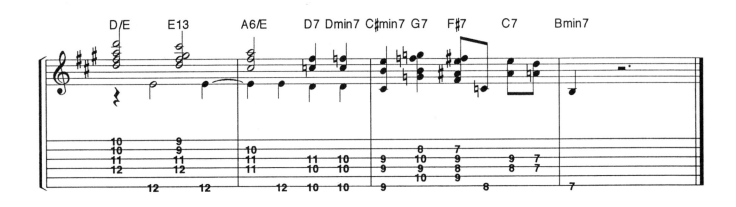

Alan de Mause

Guitarist Alan de Mause lives in New York, where he performs, writes music instruction books, and teaches both at Columbia University and at his private studio, where he also develops his *Guitar Power!* correspondence study course for students around the world. When not involved in music, Alan does computer consulting and teaches the use of software applications. Using computer-aided music sequencing and music graphics software, he provides services for musicians including arranging and the creation of lead sheets, flyers, posters, and other promotional materials.

The Chameleon

AdM

83

Joe Diorio

A master of the guitar, Joe Diorio embraces the true exploratory spirit of jazz. With over thirty years experience as a performer, recording artist, and instructor, he has worked with such jazz luminaries as Sonny Stitt, Eddie Harris, Ira Sullivan, Stan Getz, Horace Silver, and Anita O'Day, among others. In a review of one of Joe's performances at the jazz club Donte's, *Los Angeles Times* jazz critic Leonard Feather remarked: "He is one of the most mature and uncompromising new plectrists to work the room since Joe Pass."

Highly respected as an educator, Joe currently teaches jazz improvisation at the University of Southern California, and has conducted jazz guitar seminars throughout the United States, Europe, and Brazil. Joe has written five instructional books, articles for *Guitar Player Magazine's* "Master Series," and he recently completed the instructional video, *Creative Jazz Guitar*.

Joe believes that all musicians are naturally creative. In his jazz guitar seminars, he helps players unlock their full creative potential through special training exercises and techniques he has used to expand the creativity of his own playing.

Reflections of Wes

Tempo slow to medium

Diorio Original

85

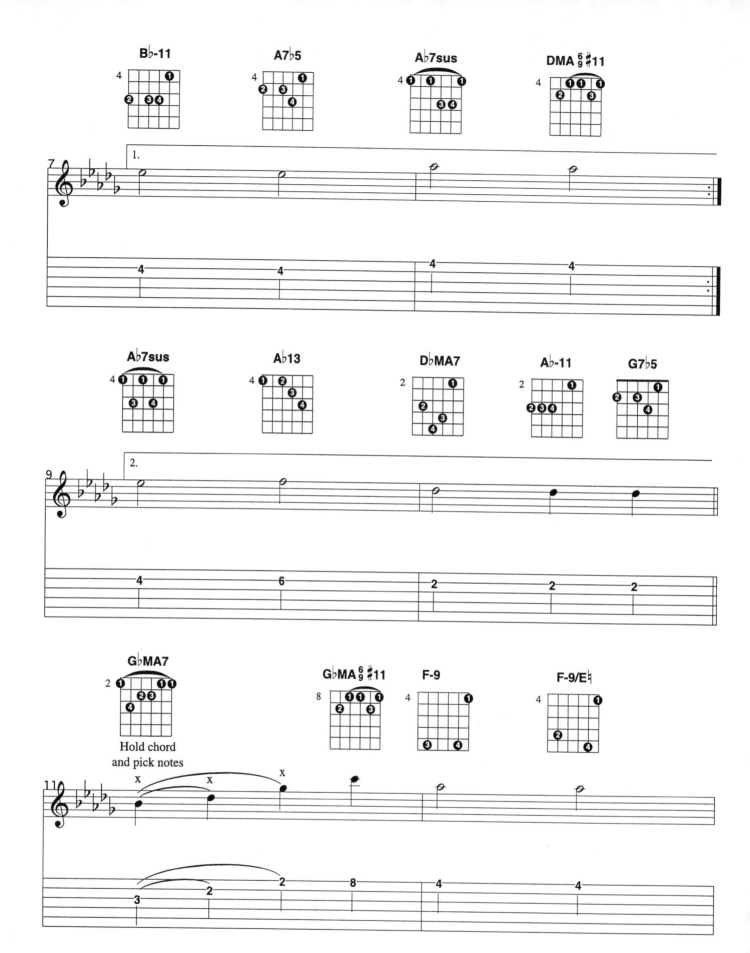

Repeat to the top and take the Coda

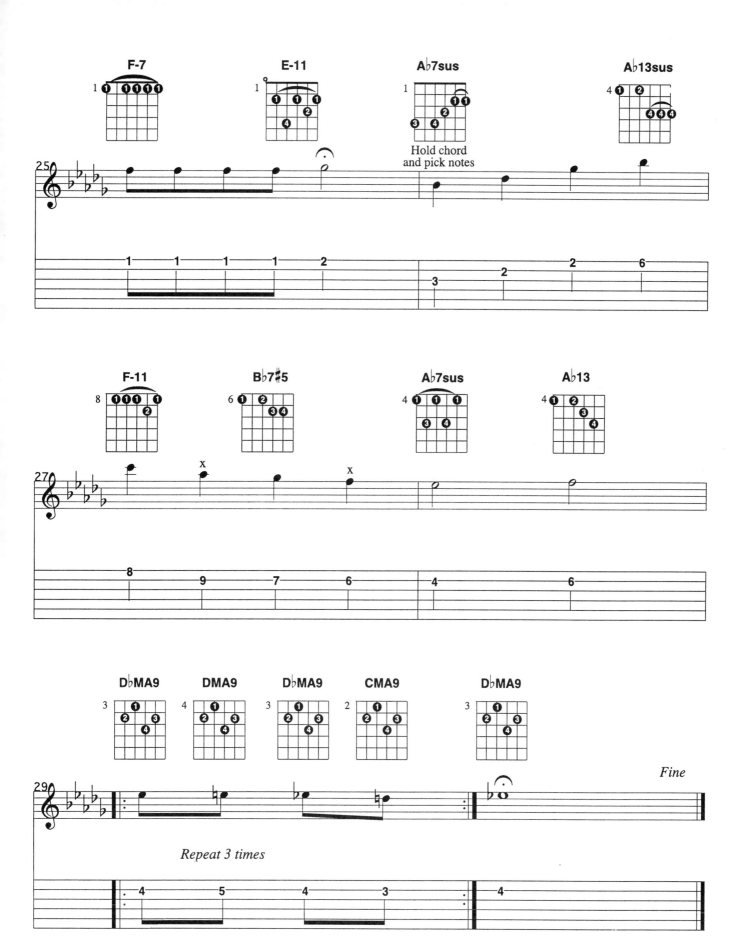

Ron Escheté

Photo by Bruce Burr

Born in 1948, Ron Escheté began playing guitar at the age of 14. While his peers were learning the music of Elvis and The Beatles, Ron was learning the likes of Jim Hall and Wes Montgomery.

After his highschool days of club work with a quartet, Escheté attended Loyola University with thoughts of a medical career, but a few months in New Orleans infected him with a love for jazz that wouldn't be deterred. After three years at Loyola, he left his study of classical guitar, and took a job on the road with Buddy Greco. In the early '70s, Escheté moved to California, and as he entered graduate school, he began teaching at the college level. Eventually he secured a position as a guitar teacher at the Music Institute of Technology in Hollywood, where he remained for many years.

As a resident guitarist in the L. A. music scene, Escheté worked in house bands on many television shows, and at live events with some of the greats of jazz, including Ray Brown, Milt Jackson, Dizzy Gillespie, Joe Diorio and Joe Pass, along with a long-standing arrangement with the Gene Harris Quartet. Escheté's list of accomplishments come, in large part, to his abilities as a world-class accompanist. He can comp like a pianist beneath his own lead lines, or integrate chords and a bass line on his trademark seven-string guitar. Although he is a strong accompanist, his melodic sense keeps him well grounded.

Homeward Bound

Latin - Fingerstyle

Ron Escheté

D.C. For Solos. Coda Last Time Only.

93

Jim Ferguson

Photo by Brad Shirakawa

In 1994, Jim Ferguson received one of the highest honors of his profession: a Grammy nomination from the National Academy of Recording Arts and Sciences in the Best Album Notes category for annotating Fantasy Records' 12-CD boxed set *Wes Montgomery—The Complete Riverside Recordings,* which includes an incisive biographical essay and interviews with numerous figures, including Nat Adderley, Ron Carter, Kenny Burrell, John Scofield, and Tommy Flanagan. The award marked a recent high point in a career that began in the mid '70s.

For more than 15 years, Ferguson was associated with *Guitar Player Magazine.* A former editor, he specialized in jazz and classical guitar—meeting, interviewing, and writing about virtually every important figure in the guitar world. A specialist in jazz, and in jazz guitar in particular, he contributed the guitar history entry and 14 biographies to *The New Grove Dictionary of Jazz.* He has also annotated over 40 albums (Wes Montgomery, Kenny Burrell, Joe Pass, Jim Hall, Tal Farlow, George Van Eps, Johnny Smith, and many others) and compiled several acclaimed collections of historic performances for the Fantasy, Rhino, and Concord labels. In addition to *Guitar Player*, his hundreds of articles have appeared in *JazzTimes, Down Beat, Classical Guitar, Fingerstyle Guitar,* and other international publications. His books have covered topics ranging from blues to the music of Federico Moreno Torroba.

A noted guitar instructor, Ferguson has a Master of Fine Arts degree from Mills College in Oakland, California, and teaches music at both Evergreen Valley College in San Jose, California, and California State University, Monterey Bay in Seaside, California. He has studied with George Barnes, Red Varner, Lenny Breau, Jose Rey de la Torre, and David Tanenbaum and performed in Europe and the U.S. Moreover, he is profiled in Maurice J. Summerfield's *The Jazz Guitar—Its Evolution, Players And Personalities Since 1900.* Regarding his own approach to jazz, *Cadence Magazine* said, "Bluesy and swinging, Ferguson bears up under repeated listening."

In 1997, Jim founded his own music publishing company, Guitar Master Class, whose first book, *All Blues For Jazz Guitar—Comping Styles, Chords & Grooves* (MB96842BCD), was received virtually with universal acclaim. In 1999, he followed that success with *All Blues Soloing For Jazz Guitar—Scales, Licks, Concepts & Choruses* (98003BCD). Both are distributed by Mel Bay. Busy with future projects, he resides in Santa Cruz, California.

Swing Low Sweet Chariot

Traditional
Arr. by Jim Ferguson

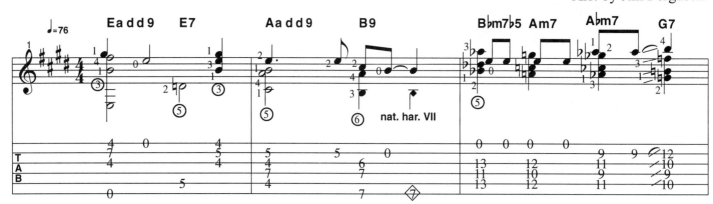
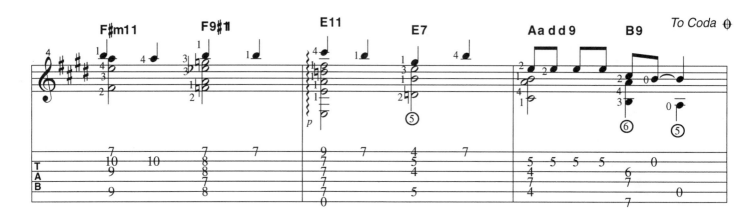
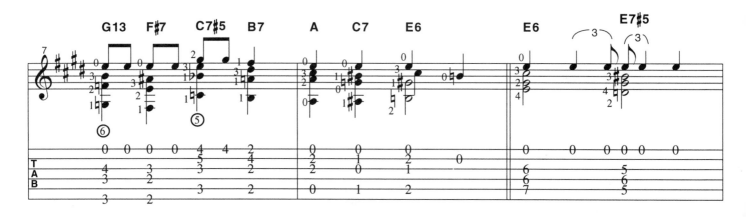
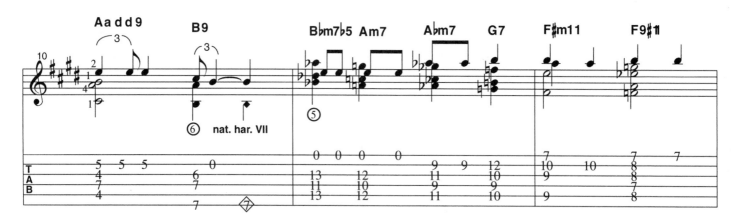

96

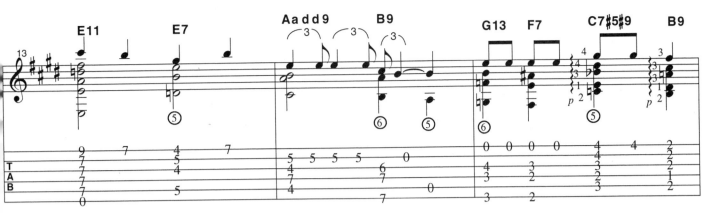

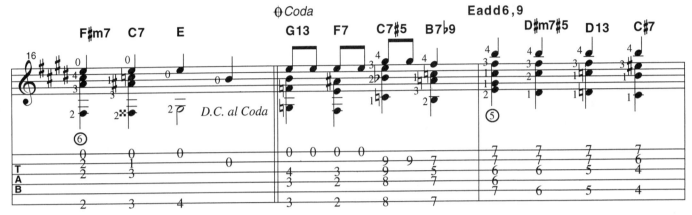

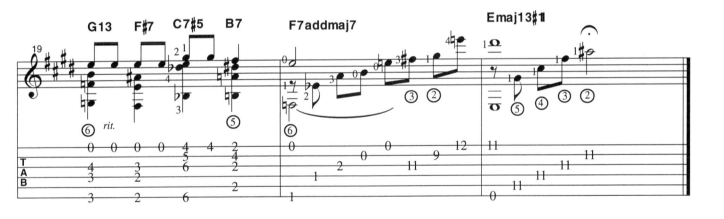

Buddy Fite

Buddy Fite's guitar style is completely unique in that once you hear him, you can always pick him out. His combination of walking bass line, rhythm and lead at the same time is almost unbelievable.

An interesting note is Buddy's approach to the guitar fingerboard. He approaches it as a keyboard player would, in that he doesn't think in terms of fret position.

* * * * * * * *

When asked about his philosophy at playing the guitar, one of the many things he will mention is that he would always learn which notes wouldn't work in a song first, then he was free to play all the others. He feels we all have the music inside and if we really listen to it, it will come out.

When asked how he got to be so good, he answers that he plays the way he does because nobody ever told him he couldn't.

-Denny Handa

Introduction *Mr. BeeBop*

99

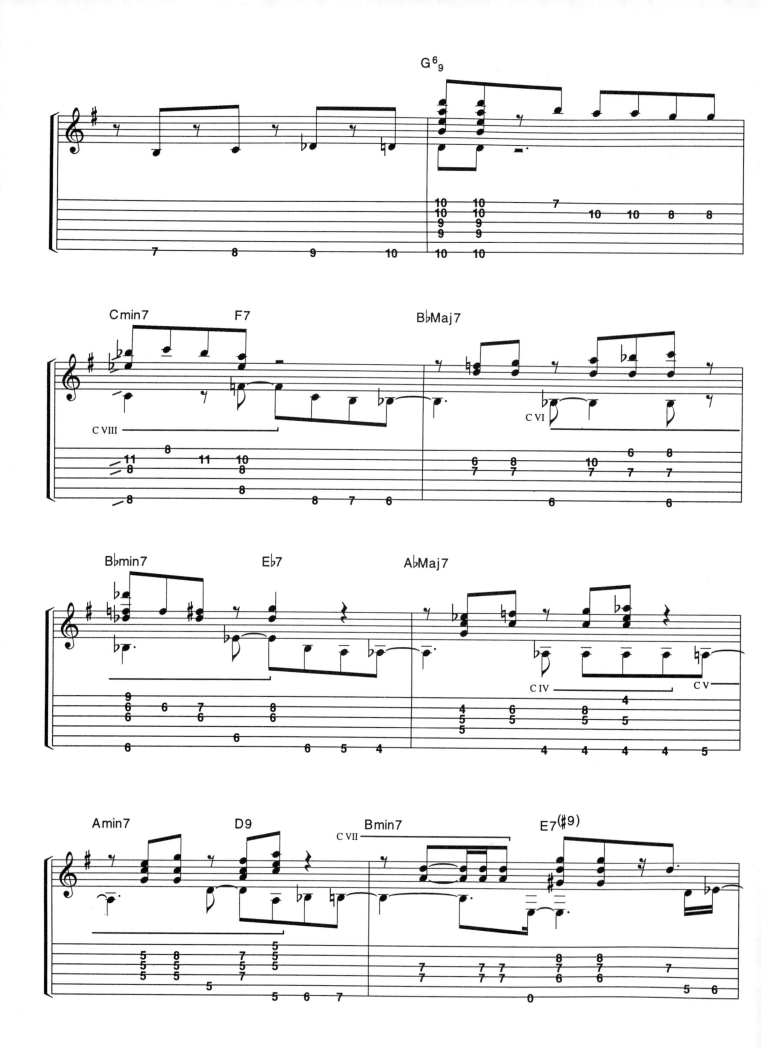

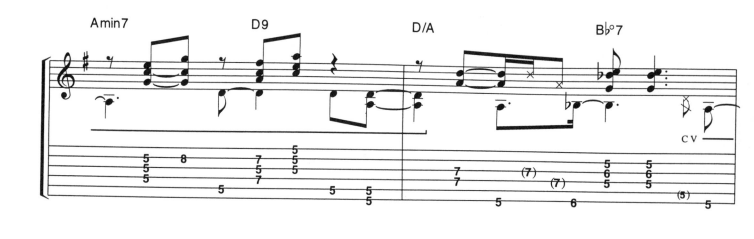

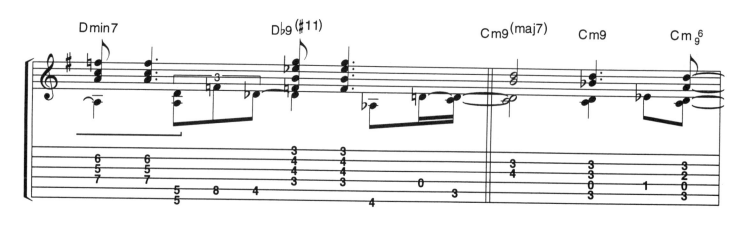

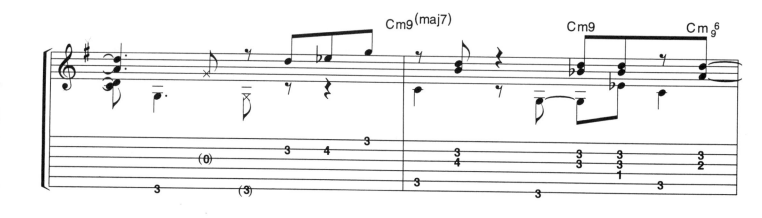

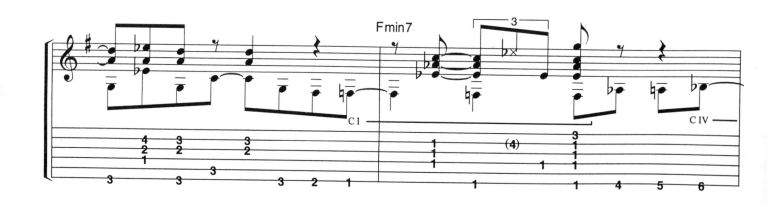

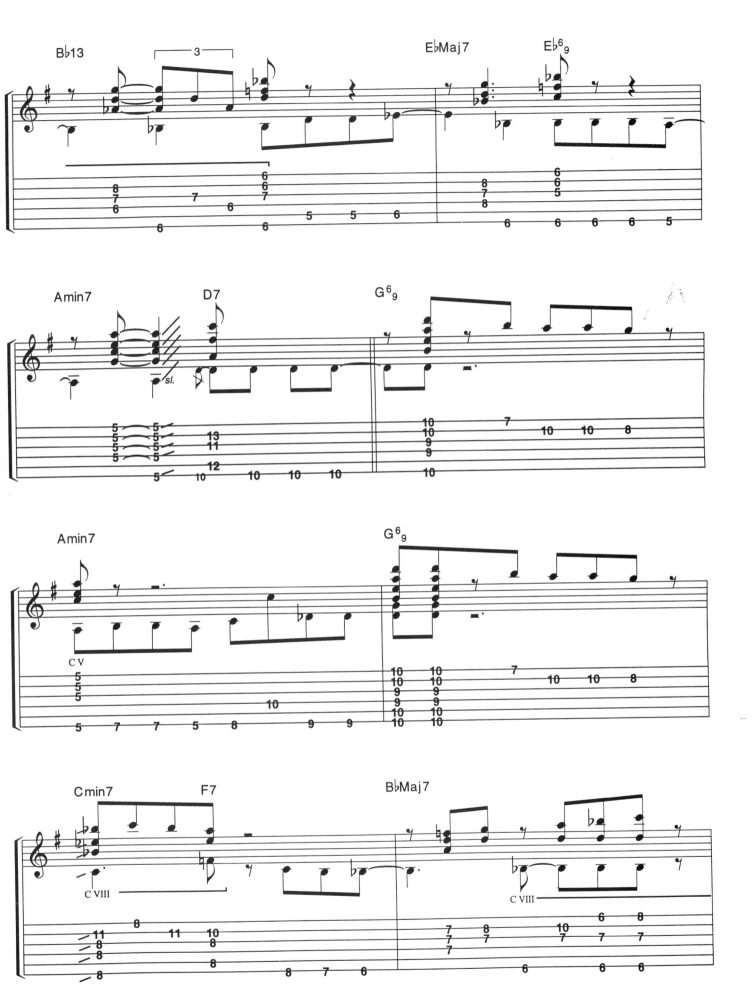

Bruce Forman

Guitarist Bruce Forman, acclaimed a "prodigious talent" by *Downbeat*, was born in 1956 and has already accumulated more that 20 years as a professional musician. Initially inspired by such guitar masters as Wes Montgomery and Joe Pass, Bruce ultimately developed his own dazzling guitar style embodying the spirit of musical freedom expressed by such be-bop wizards as Charlie Parker, John Coltrane, and Miles Davis.

A leader, as well as sideman with many of the greatest names in jazz, Bruce has performed at major jazz festivals and clubs throughout the world. Luminaries such as Bobby Hutcherson, Stanley Turrentine, Grove Washington, Eddie Jefferson, and Richie Cole have featured him in their bands.

Since 1978 Bruce has maintained an active recording career. Besides recordings of his own, he has appeared on numerous albums by other jazz stalwarts, including Mark Murphy, Lanny Morgan, Jimmy Knepper, Rare Silk, Bobby Enriquez, and many more.

Poison Ivy

Composed by:
Bruce Forman

Transcribed and typeset by:
Hemme B. Luttjeboer

Used by Permission

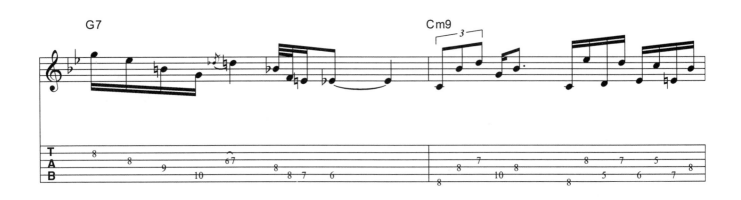

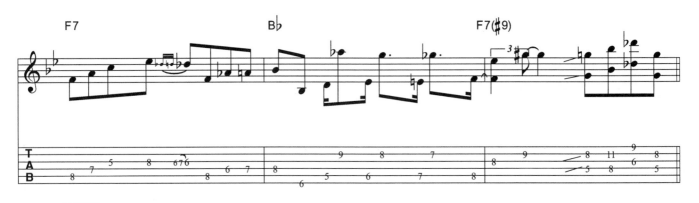

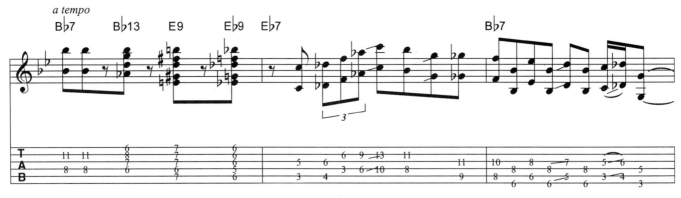

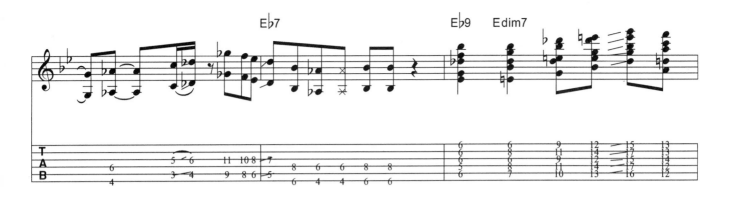

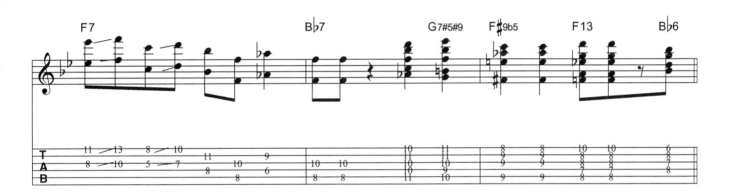

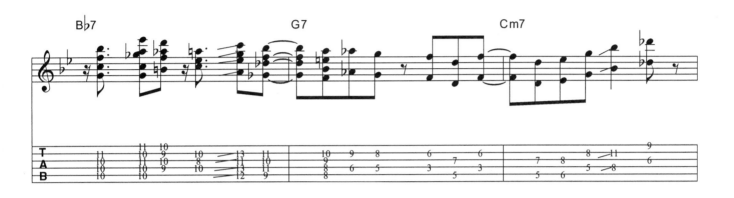

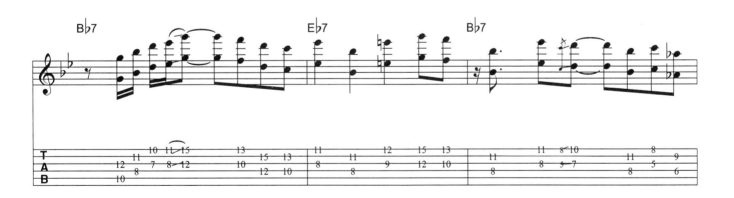

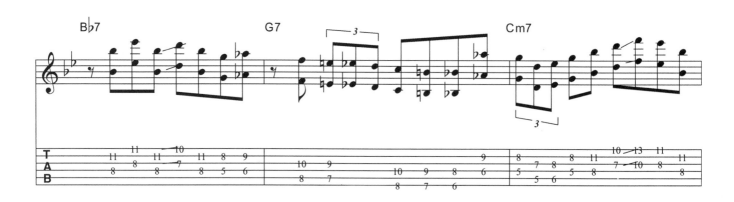

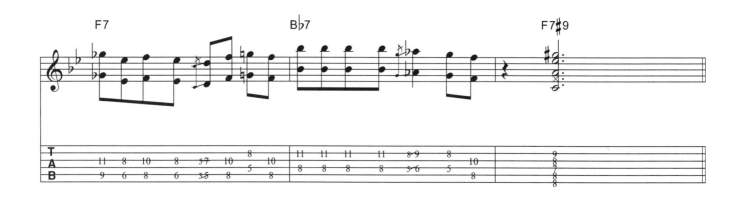

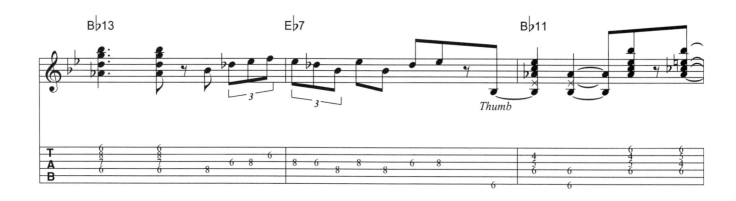

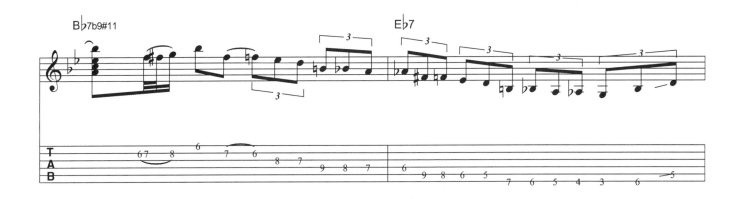

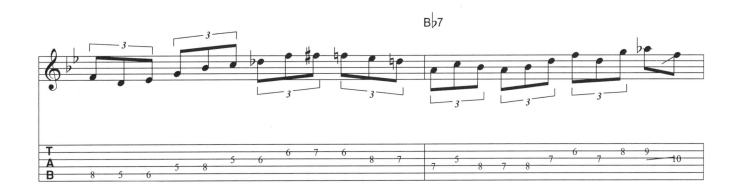

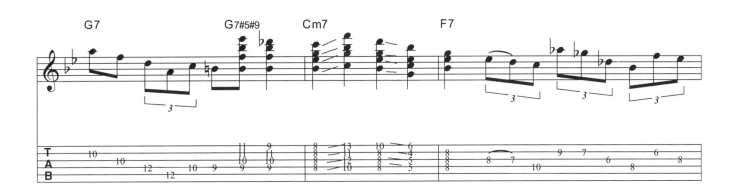

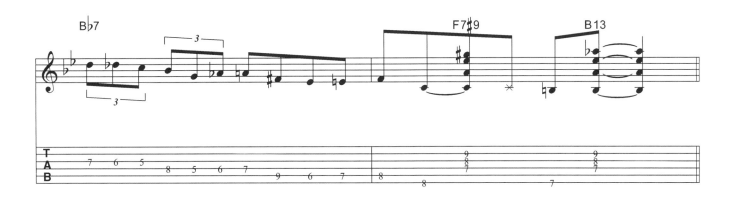

111

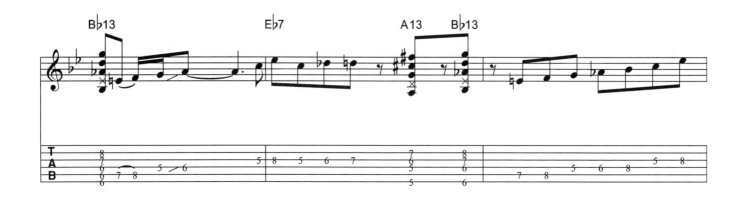

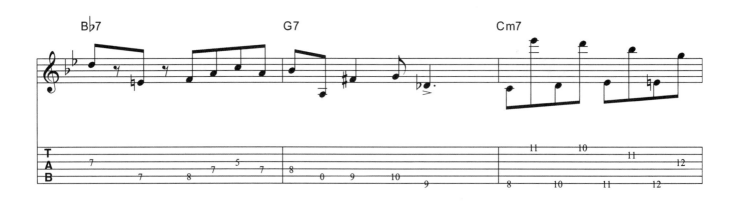

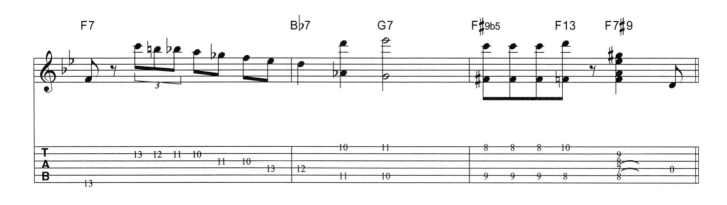

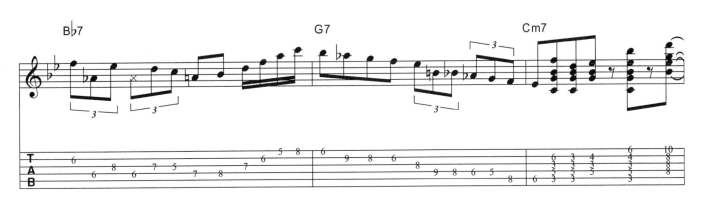

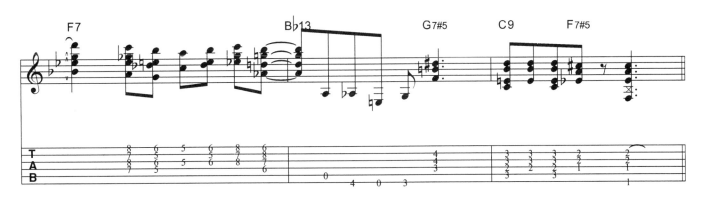

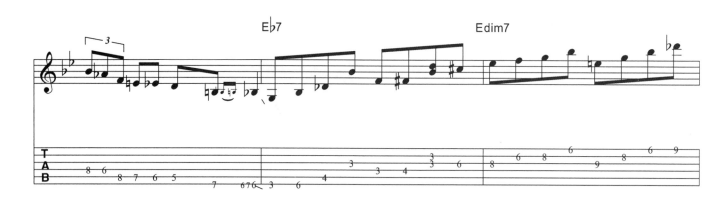

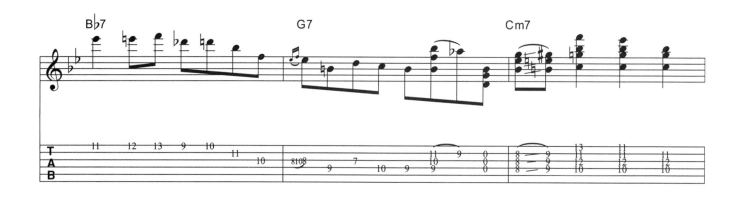

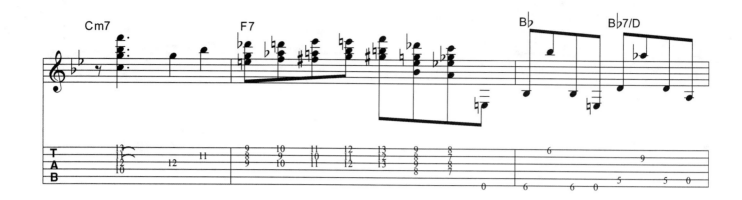

John Griggs

Since founding the Griggs School of Music in Norfolk, Virginia in 1957, John Griggs has taught thousands of pupils to play jazz and classical guitar. Many of his pupils have become teachers and world-class performers in their own right. Mr. Griggs was a guitar instructor for 20 years at Old Dominion University. He continues to teach privately, but devotes most of his energies to performing and transcribing, arranging, and composing for the guitar.

Jive Blues

Key of Bb major. Memorize and play. The form of "Jive Blues" is A-12 B-12 A-12=36 measures – 12 bar blues. The improvisation is 48 measures long with a return to A-12 to end the piece. Write and play your own blues using the chord progression of A-12. Write a blues improvisation using the chord progression of measures 25 through 36 of the written improvisation. Transpose these new blues progressions to all 12 keys and improvise on them. Write a walking bass accompaniment for "Jive Blues."

Use the Chord Structure Chart to spell the chord arpeggios. Use the Bb dorian scale with #4 for the improvisation.

Jive Blues

by: John Griggs
BMI

119

Jerry Hahn

Jerry Hahn is the director of the jazz guitar program at Portland State University in Portland, Oregon. He has recorded and toured with Paul Simon, Ginger Baker, Gary Burton, John Handy, Bennie Wallace, David Friesen and Nancy King among others. His recordings as a leader include *Time Changes* (ENJA-9007), *Jerry Hahn & His Quintet* (Arhoolie 9011) and *The Jerry Hahn Brotherhood* (Columbia). Appearances at major jazz festivals around the world include Newport, Monterey, Montreux and Berlin. Many guitarists were inspired by Jerry Hahn's Guitar Seminar, a monthly column for *Guitar Player* magazine from 1973 to 1978. The movie sound track for *White Men Can't Jump* features Jerry's guitar playing. The Jerry Hahn Contemporary Guitar Series includes *Volume 1 Scales and Exercises* (94183BCD), *Volume 2 Patterns and Solos* (94184BCD), and *Volume 3 Improvisation Course & Chord Studies* (94185BCD). All of the books come with a CD.

Down To the Wire

Jerry Hahn

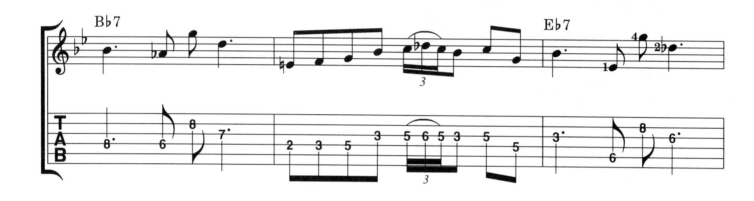

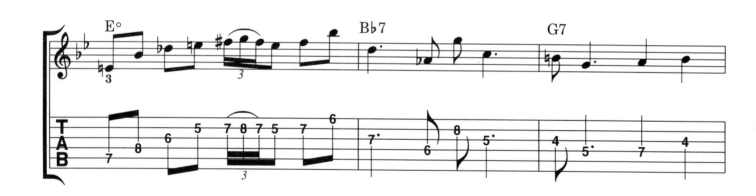

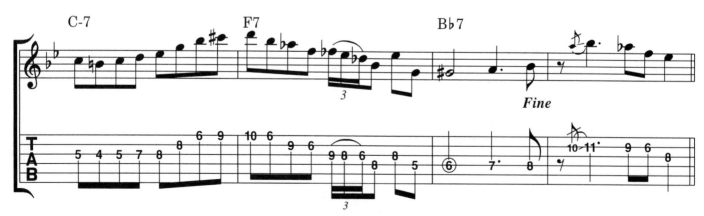

Used by Permission

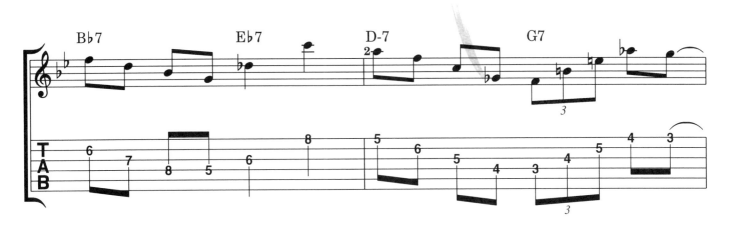

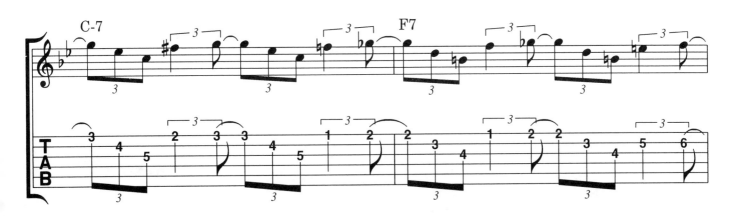

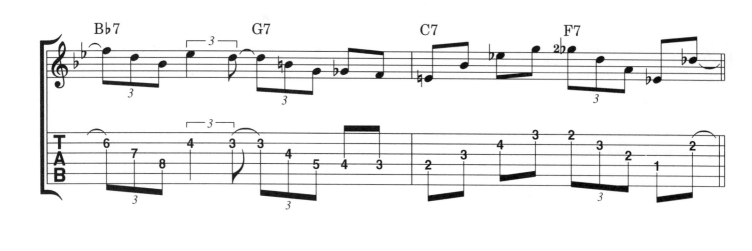

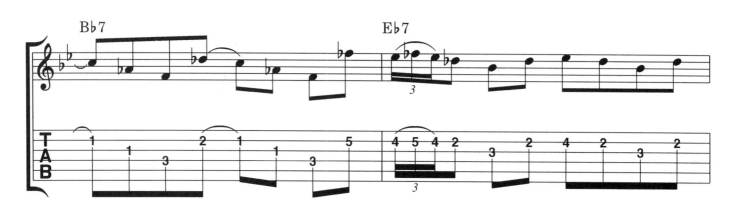

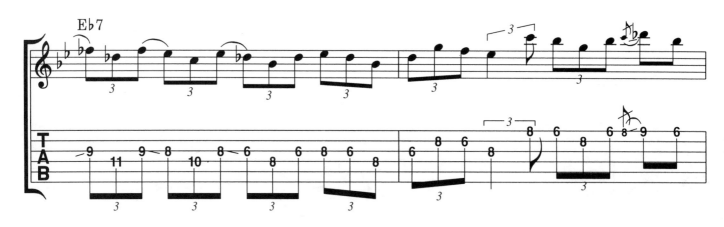

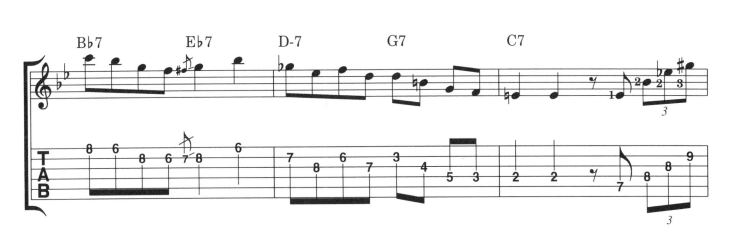

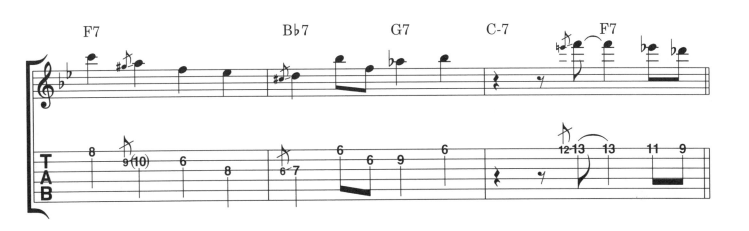

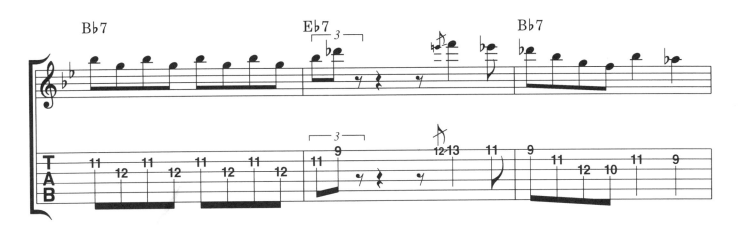

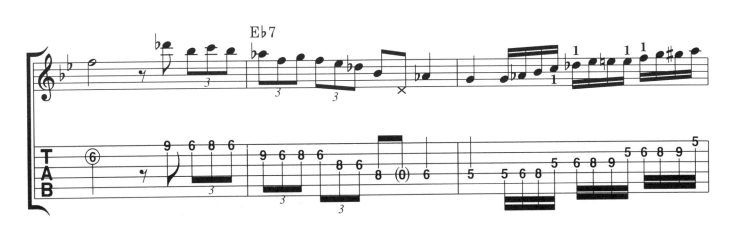

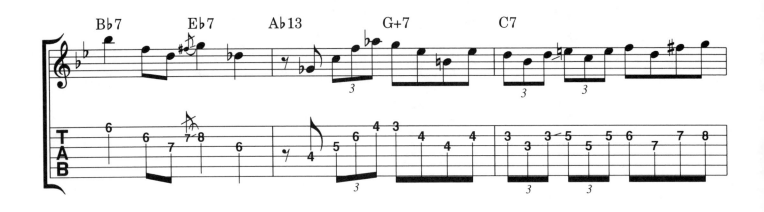

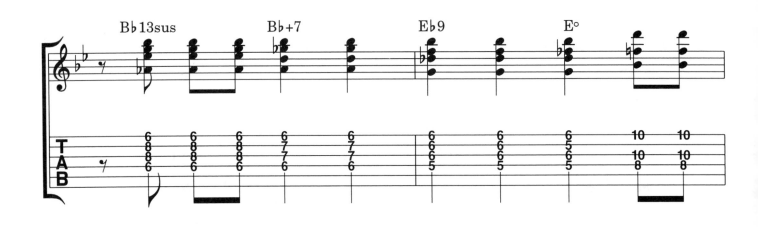

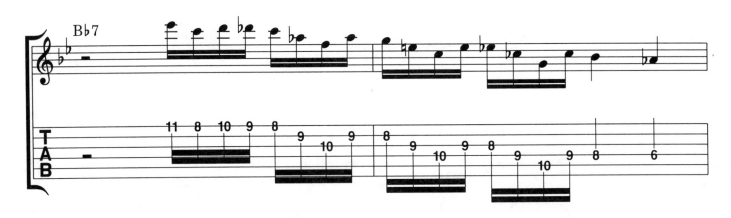

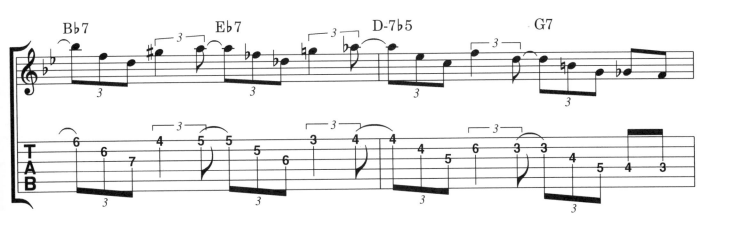

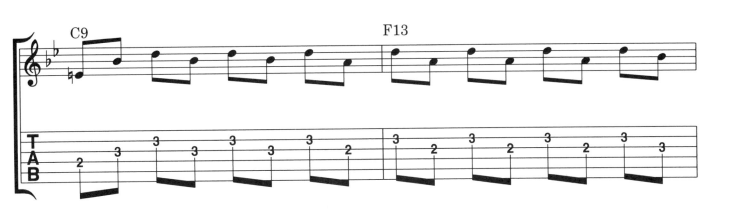

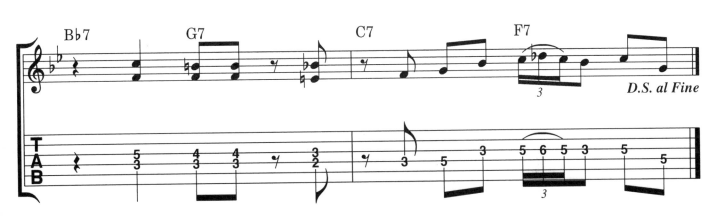

Rick Haydon

Rick Haydon is a Professor of Music at Southern Illinois University at Edwardsville where he is head of the guitar program and manages the recording studio. He teaches Advanced Jazz Improvisation, Rhythm Section Workshop, Private Applied Jazz Guitar, Supervises the Jazz Combo System, and directs the Jazz Guitar Ensemble.

Rick has been playing guitar for thirty-four years and has studied with many of the masters of jazz guitar. Among these are Johnny Smith, Howard Roberts, Pat Martino, and most recently Bucky Pizzarelli (7-string).

Professor Haydon has been performing professionally for over thirty years and has played in a variety of situations. In 1996 he performed with Herb Ellis and Mundell Lowe during the Guitar Foundation of America International Guitar Convention. He was also recently the featured artist with the Iowa State University Jazz Band. He performed with Bucky Pizzarelli before a sold out concert at the Sheldon Concert Hall in St. Louis in November of 1998.

New Folks

Rick Haydon

Used by Permission

Al Hendrickson

Al Hendrickson was born in Eastland, Texas. He became recognized as a premier jazz guitarist during stints with the Artie Shaw band and the famed Gramercy Five. Al later played with the Benny Goodman band and sextet. Known for his outstanding rhythm and chord playing, he became much sought after by leading band leaders. Al performed with Woody Herman, Johnny Mandel, Dizzy Gillespie, Louis Bellson, Ray Noble and Neal Hefti among others. Al settled in Los Angeles and became one of the busiest studio guitarists in America. He estimates that he played on over 5000 film soundtracks from 1939 to 1980! In addition, Al backed such notable musicians and singers as Frank Sinatra, Peggy Lee, Nat "King" Cole, Benny Carter, and Lena Horne. He played in orchestras led by Lalo Schifrin, Nelson Riddle and Quincy Jones.

Jazz Waltz

B.M.I.
Al Hendrickson

Roger Hudson

Born in 1961, Roger Hudson represents a new breed of classically-trained composer/ guitarist. Hudson's approach is in the spirit of composers for the guitar such as Augustine Barrios-Mangore, Fernando Sor, Mauro Giuliani, Francisco Tárrega and Leo Brouwer. All of these artists wrote as skilled composers but also as guitarists. So it is unique music that is enjoyed by guitarists and the general audience alike. The Guitar Foundation of America's journal Soundboard spoke of "...many gorgeous moments..." and "strong themes" in describing Hudson's compositions.

Hudson began playing the guitar at age 12 in the Virginia suburbs of Washington, D.C. and learned the variety of musical styles that he draws upon in his works. He has studied guitar with John Sutherland, Christopher Berg, Fred Sabback, and in master classes with Christopher Parkening. Hudson studied composition with Charles Knox and Tayloe Harding at Georgia State University where he earned a master's degree in music theory. He maintains a busy schedule of concerts, television and radio appearances, recording, composing, and is on the teaching staff at MARS in Nashville. He currently resides in Nashville, Tennessee with his wife Brenda and two children, Camille and Elijah.

Rafaela

Roger Hudson

© Roger Hudson

139

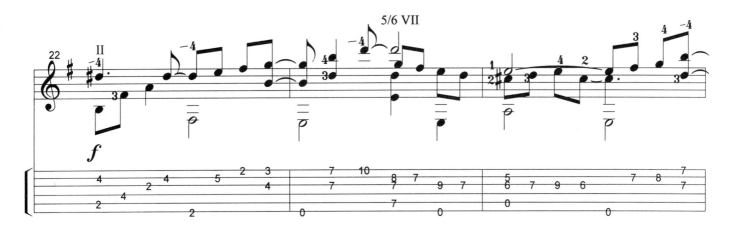

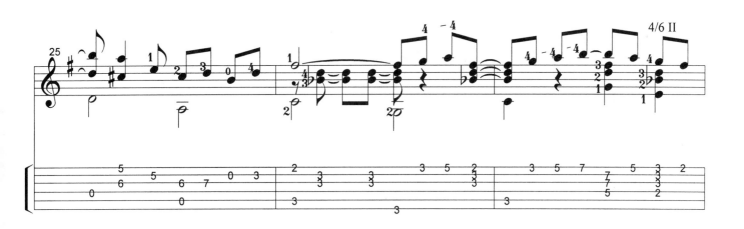

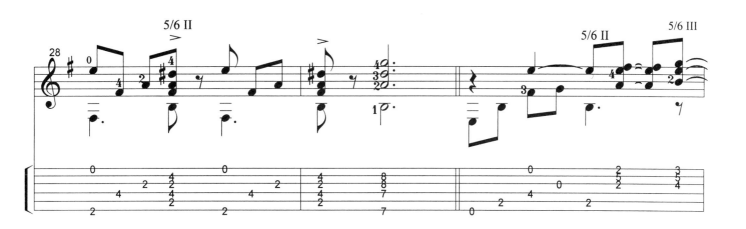

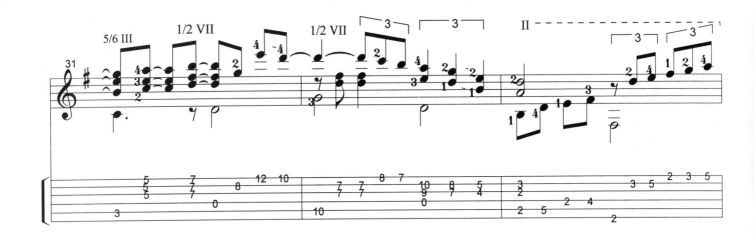

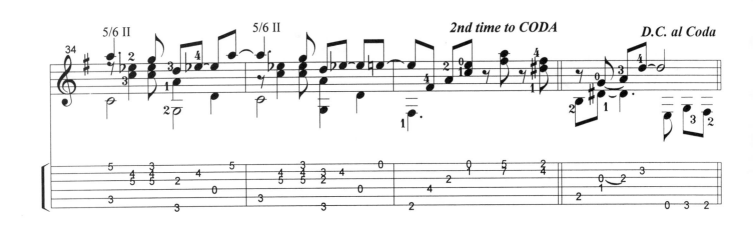

Adrian Ingram

Adrian Ingram is widely recognized as one of the foremost authorities on jazz guitar. He has written extensively on the history, players, styles and instruments of the genre. As an educator he ran the prestigious jazz guitar course at Leeds College of Music for almost 15 years, during which time he was elected a Fellow of the Royal Society of Arts (FRSA) for his outstanding contribution to music education. He holds masters degrees in music education and music performance.

"A scholar as well as a professional guitarist for over 30 years, Adrian Ingram is a respected and prolific writer...one of jazz guitar's most gifted players as well as its foremost historian."–*Bob Benedetto*

His books include the definitive biography of jazz guitarist *Wes Montgomery, The Gibson ES175 Its History and Players*, and *The Gibson L5 Its History and Players*. Adrian has produced a wide range of educational material e.g. *Modern Jazz Guitar Technique* (Hampton), *Cool Blues and Hot Jazz* (Warner Bros.) and a Suite tracing the history of jazz guitar: *Jazz Cameos* (Mel Bay.) He is also the authorized biographer of Luthier Robert Benedetto.

Adrian has written countless magazine articles and columns. He is presently columnist and consultant for *Guitarist*, Music and Reviews Editor for *Just Jazz Guitar*, and contributes to *Classical Guitar*, *20th Century Guitar*, *Vintage Guitar Classics*, *Vintage Guitar* and *Guitar*.

Dear George

Dear George is dedicated to the late great chord melody stylish George Van Eps (1913-1998). Although Van Eps played a seven string guitar for most of his professional career, he was fond of close-harmony keyboard voiced chords. Indeed, he frequently called his guitar a "lap-piano" to illustrate how much his approach had been influenced by the keyboard.

His use of vertically stacked, extended, triads was so skillfully accomplished that he made all of the difficult stretches, and wide cross-string fingerings, sound deceptively easy. Dear George is based on the piano-like chords that Van Eps loved to use. While it does feature some difficult stretches, such as those found in bars 3 and 4, 18 and 19, and 41 and 42, these can be accomplished with study and perseverance. Careful attention should be paid to the positioning of the left hand, which should be as close to a right-angle with the frets as feels comfortable.

144

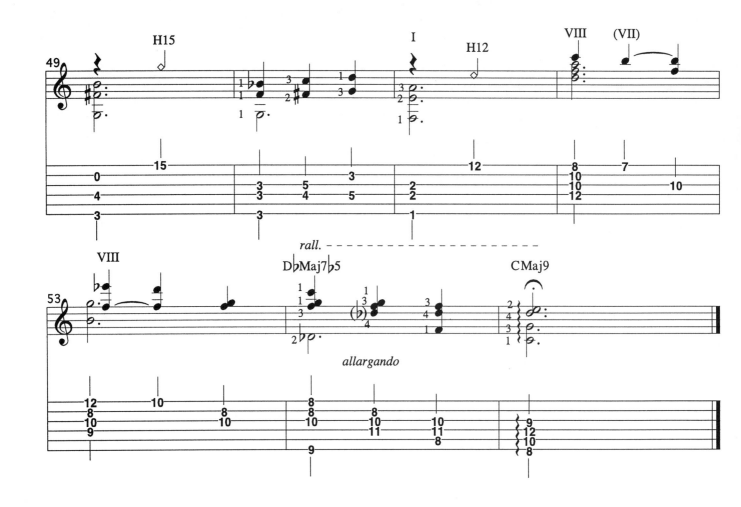

Sid Jacobs

Sid Jacobs was born and raised in Miami, Florida. When his family moved to Nevada, he obtained a position as guitar instructor at the University of Nevada, Las Vegas. This made him, at eighteen, the youngest faculty member in the school's music department.

After moving to Los Angeles he developed the curriculum for the Advanced Bebop and Jazz Guitar course at the Dick Grove School and the Jazz Guitar elective at the Musicians Institute (GIT) where he continues to teach.

In 1991, his CD *It's Not Goodnight* was released. It is a straight-ahead blowing session that features his original compositions.

Some of the jazz artists Sid has performed with include Eddie Harris, Harold Land, Buddy Montgomery, and Joe Diorio.

Reviewing a live performance, *Los Angeles Times* jazz critic Don Heckman describes him as "...a highly articulate improviser...Never at loss for a new phrase, his improvisations seemed to unfold with the ever-changing fascination of a set of Bach variations."

As an educator, Sid has made contributions to *Guitar Player* magazine, and his *Complete Book of Jazz Guitar Lines and Phrases* (MB95737) is considered to be "a thorough exploration of the modern jazz vocabulary."

Just Jazz Guitar magazine refers to Sid Jacobs as "a fine and unsung player, whose meticulous attention to improvisation is reflected in his book...I cannot praise this work too highly," and *Guitar Player* magazine says, "this package is deep."

Lullaby In Four

slowly and gently

Sid Jacobs

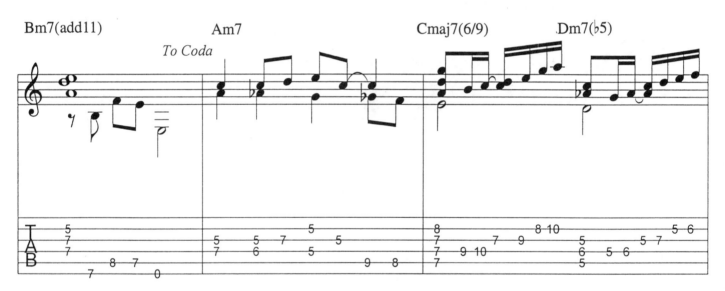

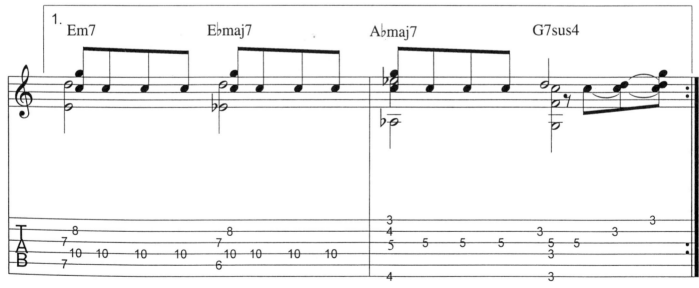

Used by Permission

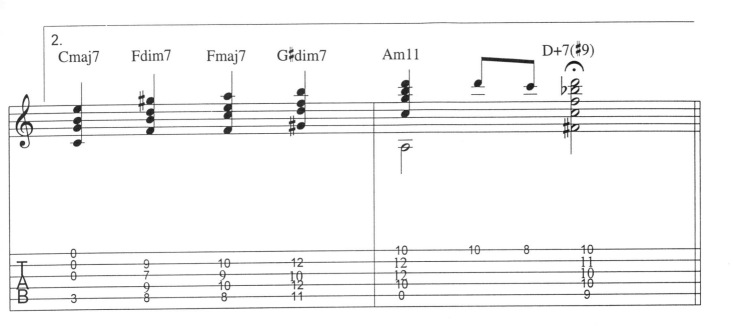

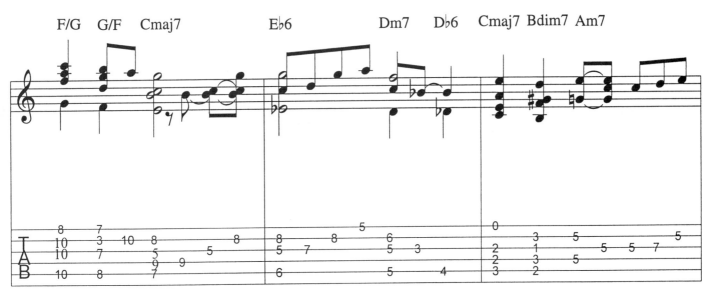

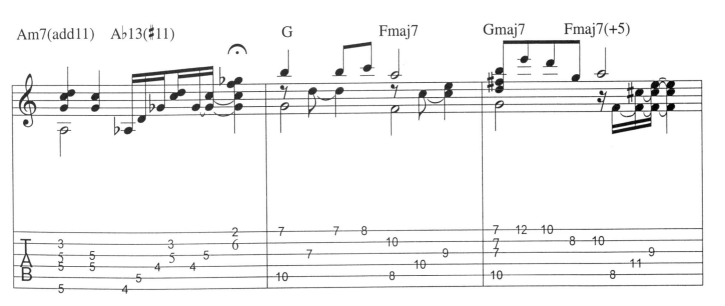

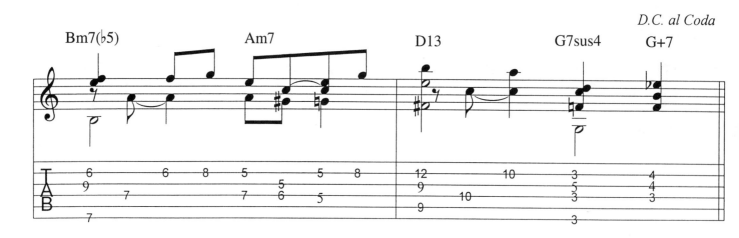

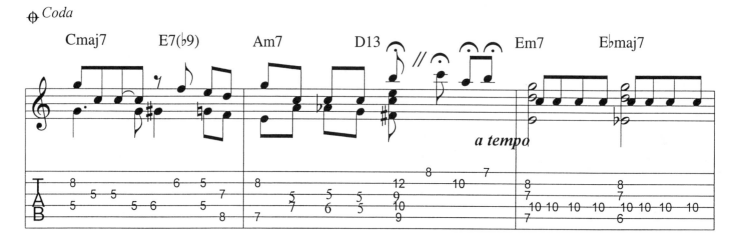

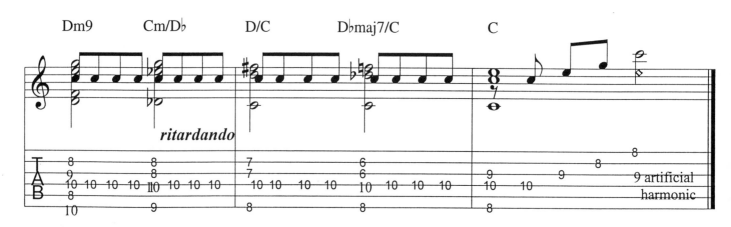

Laurence Juber

In a world filled with guitarists who gain success by mastering one style or genre, Laurence Juber is the exception–a jack of all trades, and a master of all.

As a solo artist, Juber has enjoyed a three-decade career recording and performing on acoustic, electric, classical, and 12-string guitars. He has distilled this wealth of experience into his solo concerts and guitar clinics, as well as in his original compositions.

Inspired by the explosive British pop scene of the early '60s, Juber first played an acoustic guitar at age 11. He still considers it his most personal form of expression, and has chronicled his musical experiences and influences in six collections of original acoustic guitar compositions: *Solo Flight* (1990); *Naked Guitar* (1993); *LJ* (1995); *Winter Guitar* (1997); *Mosaic* (1998); and his Narada solo debut album, *Altered Reality* (1999). Fusing folk, jazz, pop and classical styles, the albums have received rave reviews from such guitar oracles as *Acoustic Guitar, Guitar Player, Guitar International,* and *Fingerstyle Guitar.*

A native of London, England, Juber entered the music business in his early teens and quickly established himself as an accomplished and versatile musician. He was a featured soloist for the National Youth Jazz Orchestra, and earned a music degree at London University while playing guitar in such West End musicals as *Jesus Christ Superstar.* Juber became an in-demand studio player, contributing to many recording including The Alan Parsons Project, the seminal dance artist Cerrone, and the soundtrack to the motion picture *The Spy Who Loved Me.*

In 1978 Juber won an audition to become lead guitarist for Paul McCartney's Wings. He recorded and toured with group for three years, earning rave notices for his work on the hit singles *Goodnight Tonight* and *Coming Up,* and on the album *Back to the Egg,* winning a Grammy award for Best Rock Instrumental for the track *Rockestra.* After McCartney folded Wings in 1981, Juber relocated to Los Angeles area to raise a family and to concentrate on composing and studio work.

His impressive string of credits continues in California, where he has worked on countless albums, movies and TV shows with such artists as George Harrison, Ringo Starr, The Monkees, Belinda Carlisle, Air Supply, Paul Williams, and Al Stewart. Juber's playing is featured on the mega-platinum soundtrack from *Dirty Dancing* as well as in such films as *Pocahontas, Splash, The Big Chill, Ladyhawke, Shanghai Surprise, Ishtar, 1969, Lean On Me, Doc Hollywood,* and *Good Will Hunting.* His guitar is also heard on TV shows *Home Improvement, Boy Meets World,* and *Seventh Heaven.*

As a composer, Juber scored the music for the critically acclaimed Lorimar feature World Gone Wild; the BBC movie *Little Sweetheart*; the CBS movie *A Very Brady Christmas;* and the worldwide syndicated live-action TV series Tarzan. Teamed with his wife, Hope, he has recreated the score to *Gilligan's Island, The Musical,* and the repertoire of the comedy rock'n'roll group The Housewives. They recently received the prestigious Artistic Director Award from the San Fernando Valley Theater League for their children's musical *The Princess & The Frog.*

Juber, his wife, and their daughters, Nico and Ilsey, live in the Los Angeles area, where the guitarist owns a state-of-the-art recording studio.

Manhattan Snapshot

Tuning: DADGAD

Laurence Juber

Swing Feel

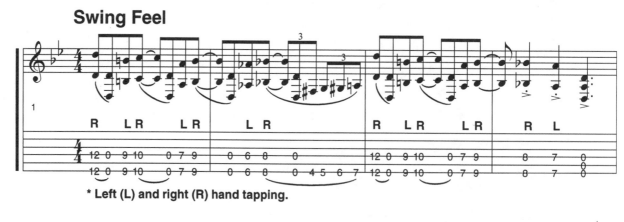

* Left (L) and right (R) hand tapping.

155

157

D. S. al Coda

159

John Lawrence

John E. Lawrence, a life long resident of Ypsilanti is one of Michigan's most talented and respected guitarists. Mr. Lawrence credits his musical talents first and foremost to God, then to the late Dr. Morris Lawrence (no relation). Dr. Lawrence was an instructor and chair of the Music Department at Washtenaw Community College (WCC). Under the tutelage of Dr. Lawrence, John was challenged and inspired to continuously improve his skills as a guitarist. Following in the footsteps of his mentor, John became an instructor at WCC where he has taught for over 20 years.

In the realm of performance, Mr. Lawrence served as musical director and lead guitarist for vocalist Carl Carlton, who was the opening act for such famed artists as Smokey Robinson, Chaka Khan, Lionel Richie and the Commodores, Rick James, Teena Marie and Frankie Beverly and Maze.

Among Mr. Lawrence's many accomplishments is a performance at Carnegie Hall. In addition to touring throughout the United States and performing at Jazz Festivals such as: The Boston Globe, The New Orleans, and Montreaux Detroit, he has performed in Haiti, Surinam, Germany, and the Montreaux Jazz Festival in Switzerland.

John has made television appearances on three nationally syndicated programs: Kelly & Company, PM Magazine and Good Morning America. He has also performed with Atlantic Records recording artists, Straight Ahead, a Detroit-based female jazz group.

One of Mr. Lawrence's most memorable occasions was with legendary jazz guitarist, Mr. Kenny Burrell. Mr. Burrell asked John to sit in with him at the famed Baker's Keyboard Lounge in Detroit, Michigan. After the performance, Kenny commended John on his playing ability.

His sound recordings include, *Merry Christmas from John E. Lawrence*, *The Supreme Dream* and *Old Smooth*. His latest project entitled *Summer Nights* is all original material that fits the adult contemporary smooth jazz format, scheduled for release in January 2000. These accomplishments have laid the foundation for an explosive career in today's music industry.

Home

(Transcribed by Joe Palmer)

Written by John E. Lawrence
[Copyright] 1999

Used by Permission

Jeff Linsky

Through his many concerts and workshops throughout the United States and abroad, Jeff Linsky has established his place in the guitar world. "This astonishing guitarist," writes *Acoustic Guitar Magazine,* "seems to have bridged entirely the troublesome gap between brain and fingers." *Guitar Player Magazine* writes: "Linsky freely improvises chord-melody solos that are frequently as brilliant as the most finely honed composition. He has met one of the greatest challenges in the guitarists' universe–and made it look easy."

As a composer, arranger, and bandleader, Jeff has earned critical acclaim for his stellar recordings. The 1989 release, *Up Late* (Concord Picante), features "a blockbuster line-up that gives forth with a sound that is intuitive, fresh, and exhilarating. A must have!" according to *Jazzscene Magazine. Simpatico* (Kamei) was nominated "Best Contemporary Jazz Recording" of 1991 by the National Association of Independent Record Distributors. Of the 1992 solo guitar project, *Solo* (GSPJAZ), *Acoustic Guitar Magazine* writes: "Finally, a recording captures this virtuoso at his effortless best," while *Jazzscene Magazine* named *Solo* in their top ten jazz CD's for 1992. And the very popular *Rendezvous* (Kamei) was among the most played recordings on the jazz airwaves in 1993. Jeff has recently returned to the Concord Picante label, and has recorded a new CD with his group, scheduled for release in the summer of 1994.

A native of Southern California, Jeff began playing the guitar at the age of ten. Although primarily a self-taught musician, he did study briefly with several notable guitarists, including the Spanish guitar virtuoso Vicente Gomez and jazz great Joe Pass. Jeff's love of improvisation and interest in many styles of music has led to collaborations with a wide variety of artists, as well as an active concert and recording career, both as a soloist and leader of his own group, with numerous radio and television appearances to his credit. Aside from concerts and recording, Jeff also writes music for film, having most recently scored the music for a World of Audubon prime-time television special for TBS.

The Love Club

CAPO, third fret
medium

Jeff Linsky

165

Dennis McCorkle

A few years ago, I was chosen as one of the top five hundred 'New Age' musicians in the world by Macmillian Press. Although I'm very pleased to be recognized for the music that I have written, I am more pleased to have had the opportunity to have music, and my modest gift for it, play such an important role in my life. It has always brought me great pleasure.

I'm also pleased that so many people have enjoyed the work that I've done throughout the years. Since the early sixties, when I left the piano and went onto playing and studying guitar, I have written more than fifty compositions and transcriptions for the instrument; numerous works for voice, orchestra, and concert band; and various instructional methods.

As a formally trained musician in both classical music and jazz, I have had some very fine teachers along the way including Frank Mullen, John Marlow and Dennis Sandole. Under their tutelage and influence I have developed a style that I believe, combines both idioms. During the past thirty years, I have performed regularly as a solo guitarist and studio musician in the Washington, DC, Atlantic City and New York areas.

Just For the Thinking

170

171

Paul Mehling

Paul Mehling is the founder and lead guitarist of the Hot Club of San Francisco, a group dedicated to performing and recording the music known as Gypsy Jazz. An accomplished multi-instrumentalist (guitar, violin, bass, plectrum and tenor banjo, mandolin), Paul has been a professional musician for over 25 years. As a member of Dan Hicks' Acoustic Warriors, he appeared on Austin City Limits, among other venues throughout the country. Internationally known as an authority on the music of Django Reinhardt and other Gypsy swing players, Paul conducts clinics and private lessons when not performing and recording with the Hot Club.

Swing This

Medium Swing

♩ = 208

Paul Mehling

173

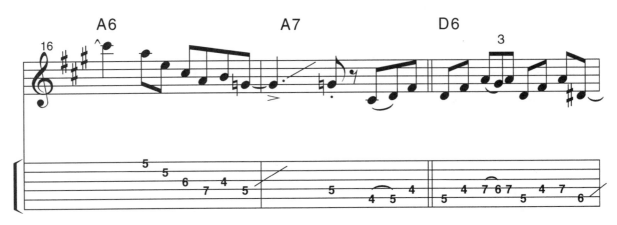

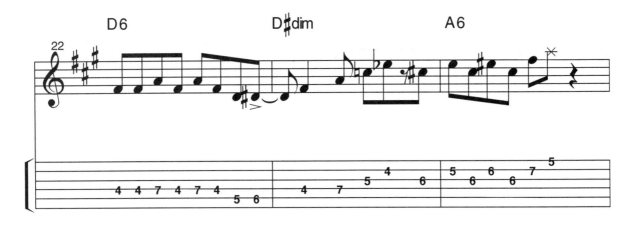

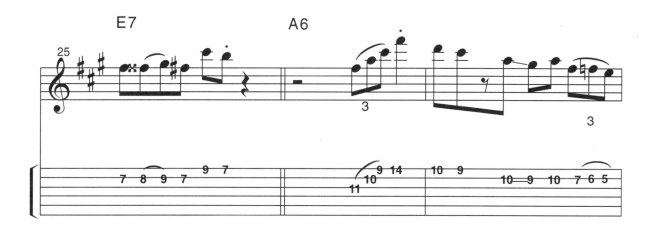

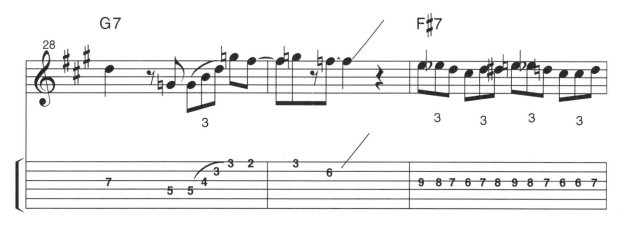

Bill Moio

Bill Moio was born and raised on the east coast, picked up his first guitar at the tender age of eight and made his professional debut at fifteen years old. After finishing high school, Bill was accepted to the prestigious Berklee College of Music in Boston, Massachusetts, where he studied under the late William G. Leavitt.

After leaving Berklee, Bill returned home to Maine and began teaching guitar at the University of Maine at Augusta. It was at this time that Bill founded his first group "The Bill Moio Quartet." The group performed an eclectic blend of jazz, Latin and funk music, hilighted by Bill's fiery guitar playing.

1979 found Bill heading west for a two-week engagement at the MGM Reno; the two weeks turned into nine months as he found himself immersed in the showroom circuit throughout Nevada. Bill served as house guitarist for Harrah's Reno and Harrah's Lake Tahoe for seven years. He held down the position of orchestra leader for Harrah's Tahoe for two years.

Bill has performed with legendary soul band Tower of Power. He also has appeared with jazz and contemporary jazz artists, Marc Russo, Richard Elliot, Bill Waltrous, Nelson Rangell and Joe Diorio to name a few.

Currently Bill has just released his newest solo project entitled, *Let's Go*. The CD showcases Bill's phenomenal guitar playing, writing and arranging. Featuring well crafted originals and fresh takes on the classic standards, *Angel Eyes* and *My One And Only Love*.

Time Stood Still

Bill Moio

♩ = 92   6th String tuned to D

Used by Permission

Play Freely

178

179

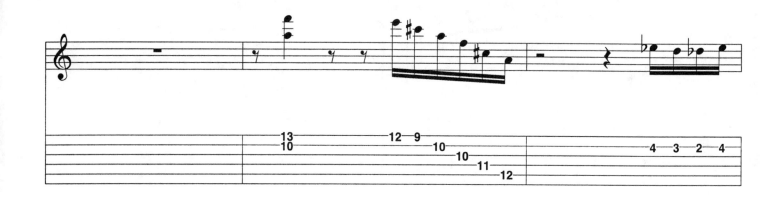

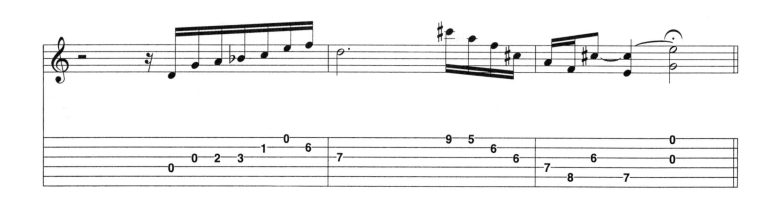

Flippin' With Bird

Bill Moio

♩ = 110 Based on rhythm changes

Used by Permission

185

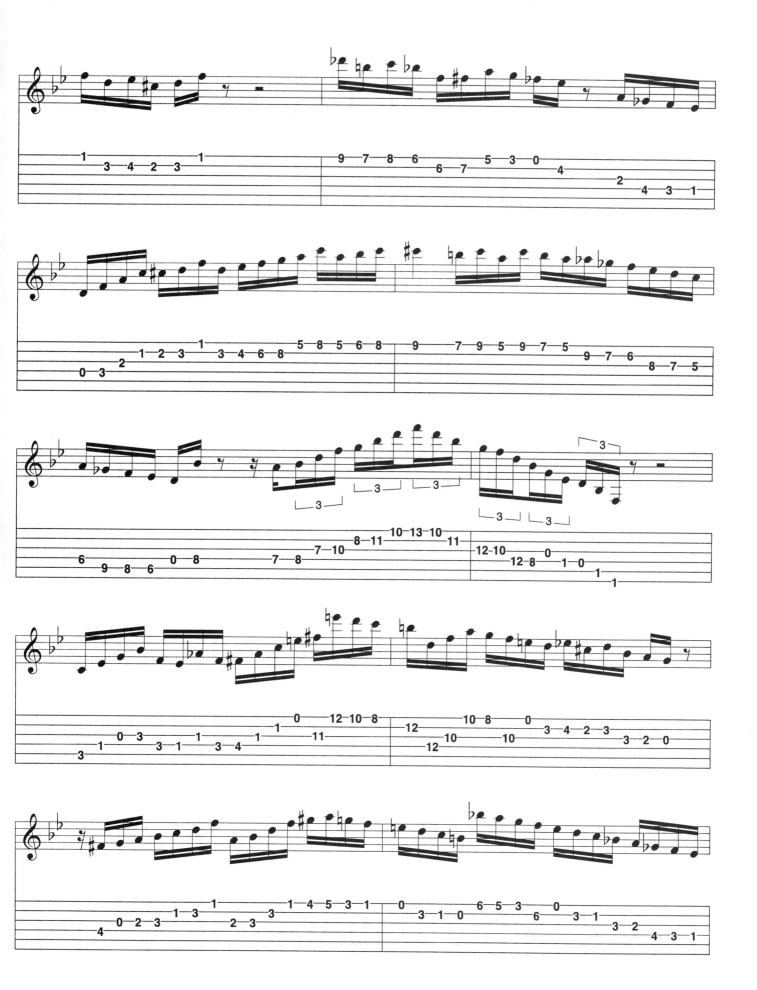

187

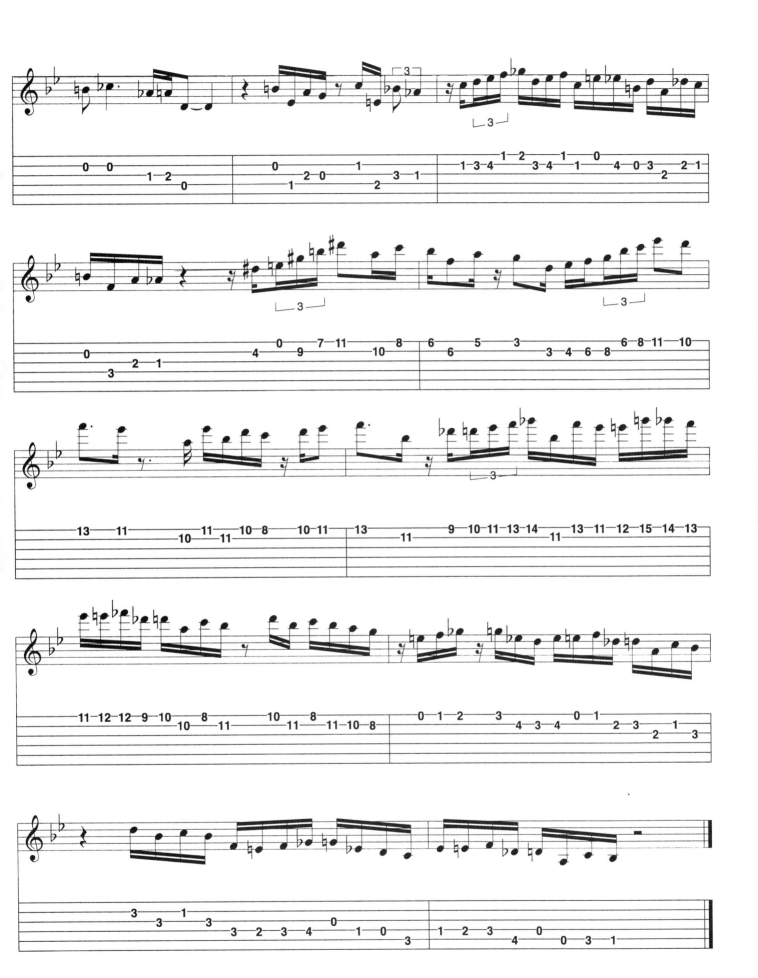

Van Moretti

Van Moretti was born in 1919 in Pen Argyl, PA. His first guitar teacher was one of the Martin brothers from Martin Guitars. He studied guitar and arranging for four years with guitarists Watts Clark in Bethlehem, PA. After serving in the Army band and traveling Europe during the second world war, he settled in New York in 1946 and worked as a freelance guitarist. He played with pianist Jan August from 1948-1950 and then opened his studio in Manhattan across the street from Radio City Music Hall, where he taught until 1979. During those years he played TV, radio and Broadway shows as well as performing at the Waldorf Astoria's Peacock Alley. He has written a chord Melody system book which is still available and contributes arrangements to *Just Jazz Guitar* magazine. Van continues to teach selected students at his home in New Jersey.

Swingin' On 7

Play notes on the 5th string
on the 7th string since
they are both tuned to A

Music by Van Moretti

Moderate swing

Howard Morgen

Howard Morgen, seven string guitarist, arranger and clinician has written fingerstyle jazz columns and arrangements for *Guitar Player, Guitar World, Acoustic Guitar* and *Just Jazz Guitar* magazines and is currently a columnist for *Fingerstyle Guitar* magazine. His most recent CD release is called *Howard Morgen Plays Gershwin*. In addition, Howard is the author of *The Gershwin Collection for Solo Guitar, The Ellington Collection for Solo Guitar, Howard Morgen's Solo Guitar Insight, Preparations: An Introduction to Fingerstyle Playing, Concepts: Arranging for Fingerstyle Guitar, 10 from Guitar Player, Fingerstyle Favorities* (Warner Bros.), *Paul Simon for Fingerstyle Jazz Guitar* (Amsco Publ.) and *Fingerstyle Jazz Images for Christmas* (Mel Bay, MB94409). He has been a guest artist/teacher during Jazz Week at the National Guitar Summer Workshop in Connecticut (1995-1997) and is currently on the faculty at the Guitar Study Center of the New School in Manhattan and the Jazz Study Program at C. W. Post Campus, Long Island University. His bio is included in Maurice Summerfield's *The Jazz Guitar, It's Players and Personalities Since 1900*.

Ohhh! Susanna

Stephen Foster
Arr. Howard Morgen

Standard Tuning

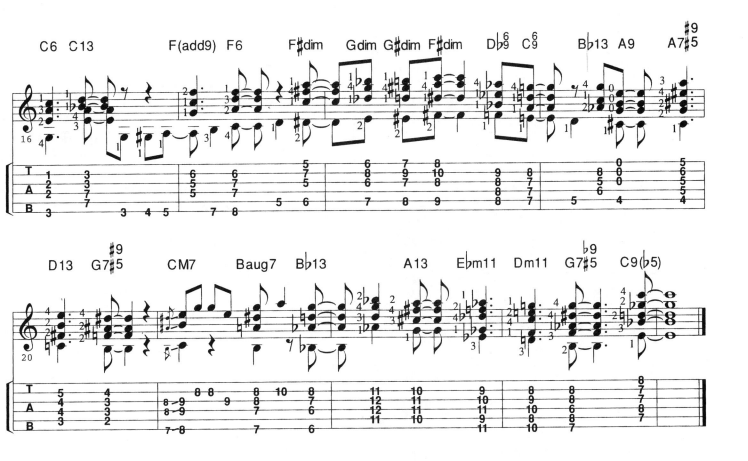

Ronald Muldrow

Born in swinging Chicago, Ronald Muldrow's first vivid experience of live music came at a very early age. Ronald remembers, "My mother took me along to the show at the Regal theater. I was very excited because I had never seen music played live. The band that opened the show played Three Blind Mice as their first tune. I didn't understand what they were playing, but I knew that tune. Their shiny horns under the colored lights made it all the more a magical experience. Later I learned that the band I heard was Art Blakey's Jazz Messengers."

During a hospital stay in his teens, he heard Wes Montgomery playing Canadian Sunset on the radio. "I hadn't been listening to jazz up to that point; I would not have a clue as to what instrument Wes was playing if the DJ had not announced that was Wes Montgomery on guitar." Ronald's subsequent influences on guitar include Kenny Burrell, Grant Green, and Phil Upchurch.

Ra-Fe-El

Ronald Muldrow

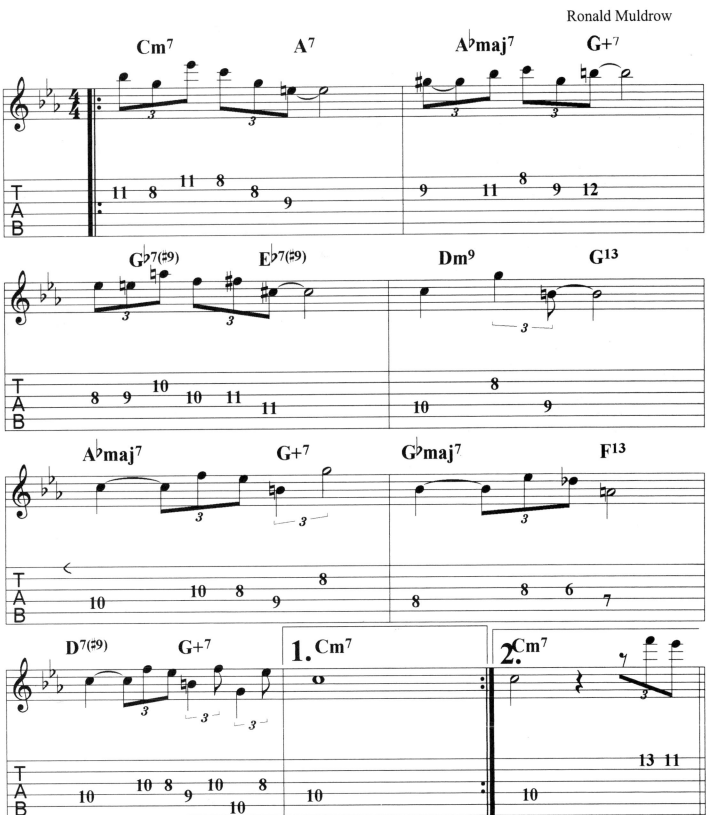

Soleshia Music 1998

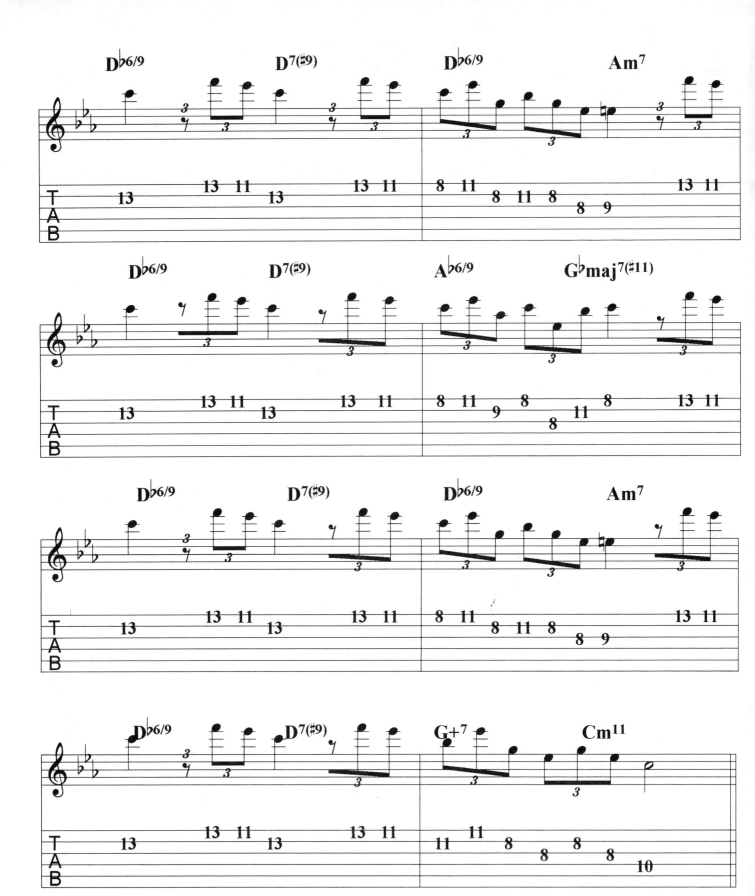

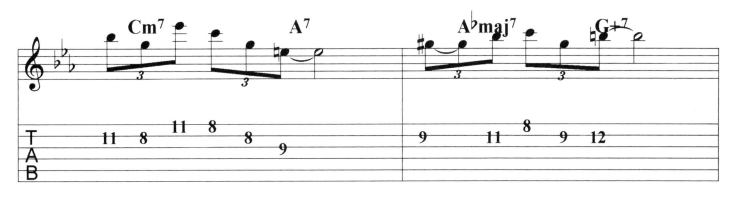

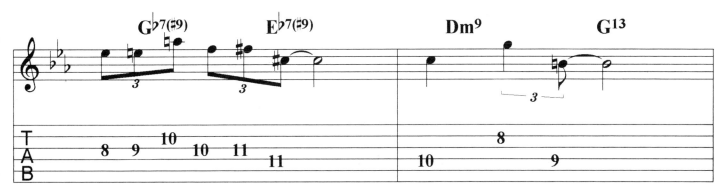

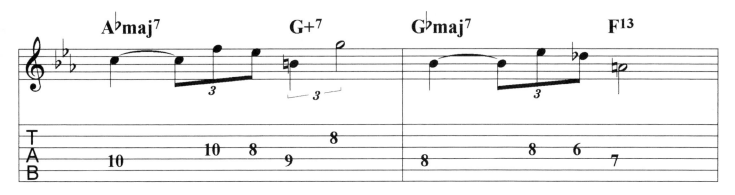

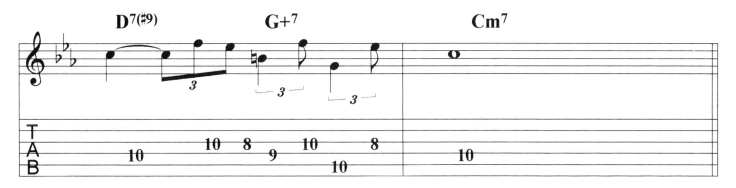

solo

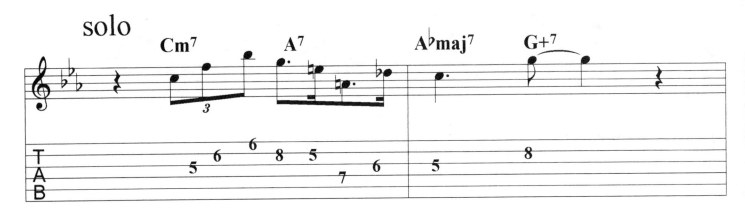

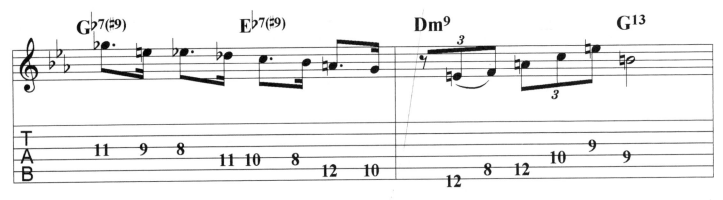

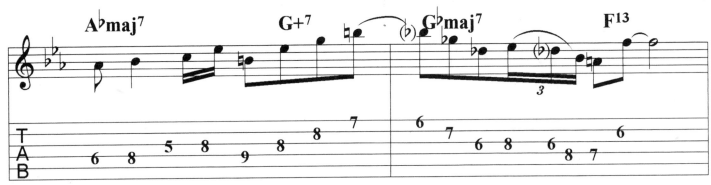

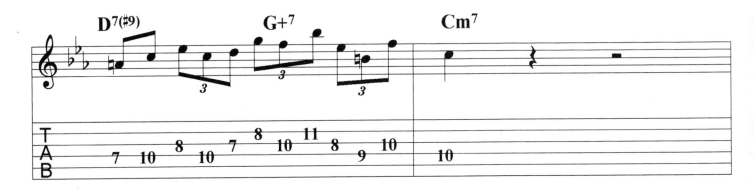

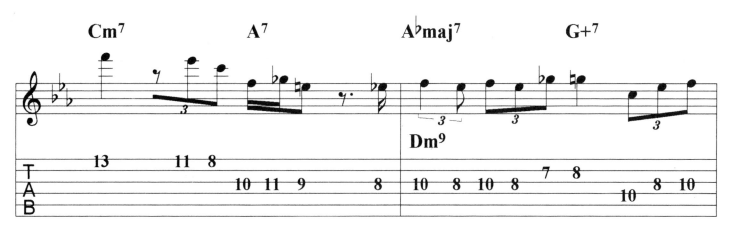

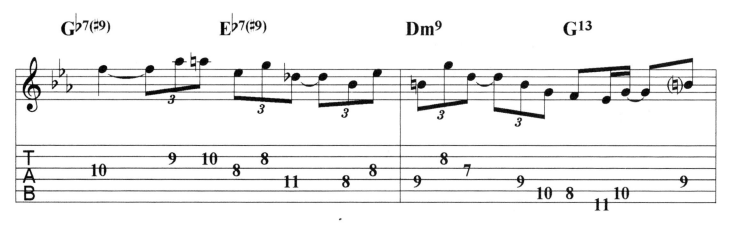

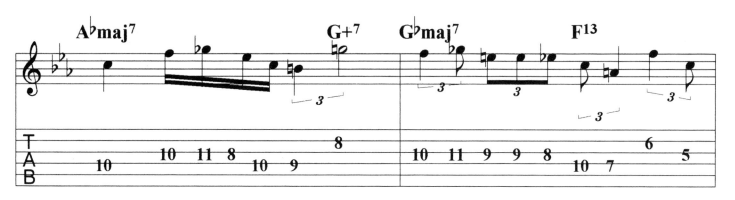

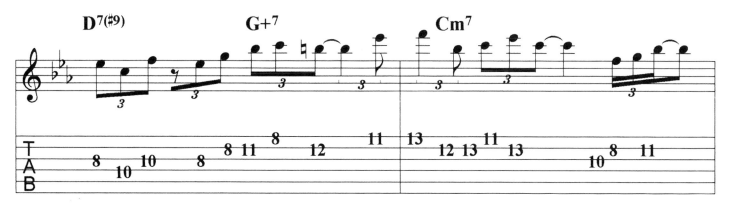

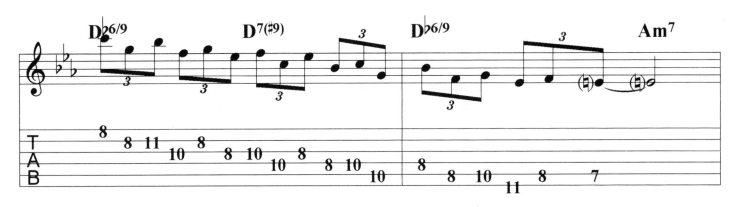

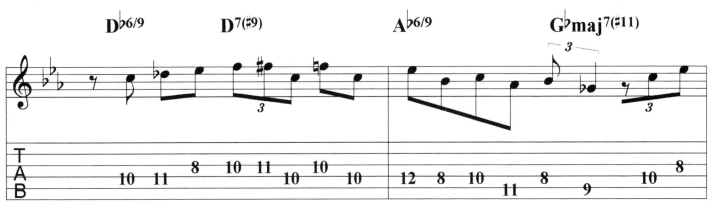

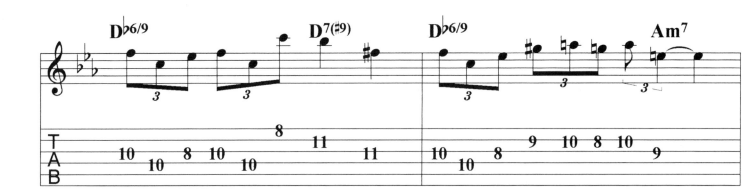

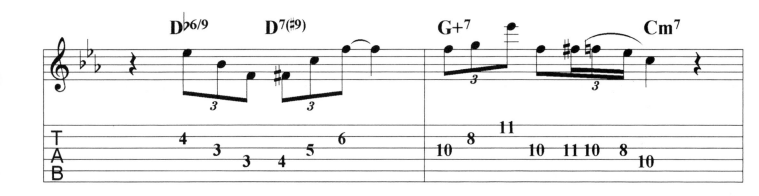

Paul Musso

Paul Musso is a professor of music at the University of Colorado at Denver. He has been with U.C.D. for nine years teaching jazz guitar improvisation, fretboard theory and applied guitar studies. Paul is also an honorarium instructor at the Community College of Denver where he has been teaching music theory, music history, music on the computer and guitar studies for the last six years. Mr. Musso is a freelance guitarist and has performed throughout the Colorado area in many diverse musical settings including the Colorado Symphony, The Boulder Festival Orchestra, The Aspen Music Festival and The Westcliff Jazz Festival. Paul is the author of two other Mel Bay Publications; *Fingerstyle Jazz Guitar — Teaching your Guitar To Walk* (MB95376BCD) and *Graded Fingerstyle Jazz Guitar Solos* (MB97168BCD). Paul has also published articles in *Fingerstyle Guitar* magazine. Paul currently lives in Denver where he maintains a career playing guitar in straight-ahead jazz and solo guitar settings.

Moon Flower

Moon Flower is based on modal latin jazz tunes like "Little Sunflower." The bass line utilizes a continuous pulse while the melody is harmonized in fifths. Pay close attention to the separation of the bass and melody, a "two guitar" sound can be achieved.

Moon Flower

Latin

♩= 120   6=D

Dm13

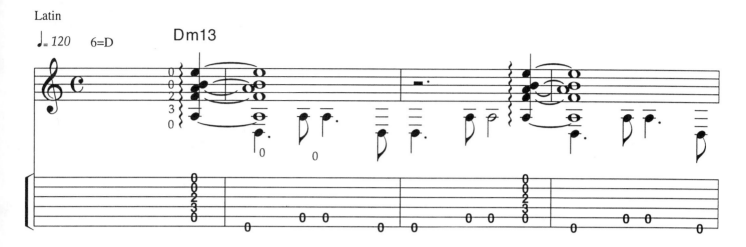

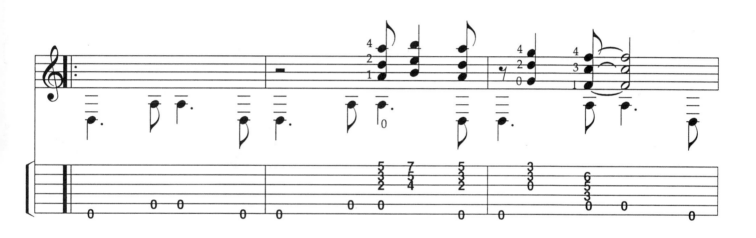

Dsus4   Dm

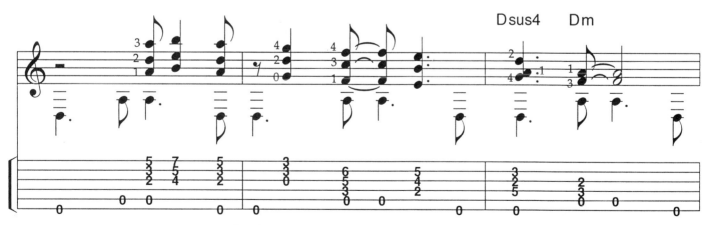

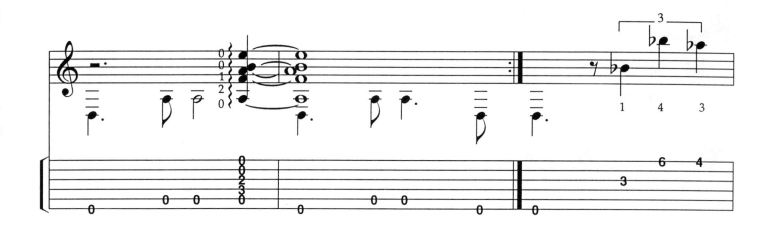

Ebmaj7

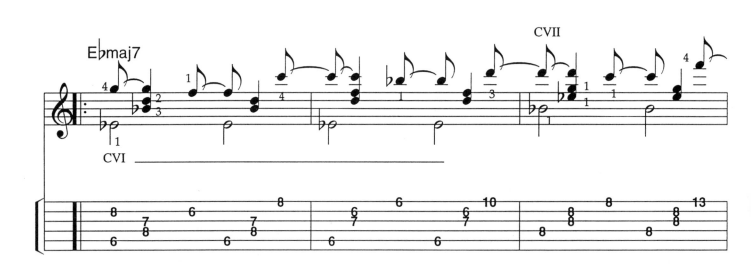

CVI _____

Dmaj7

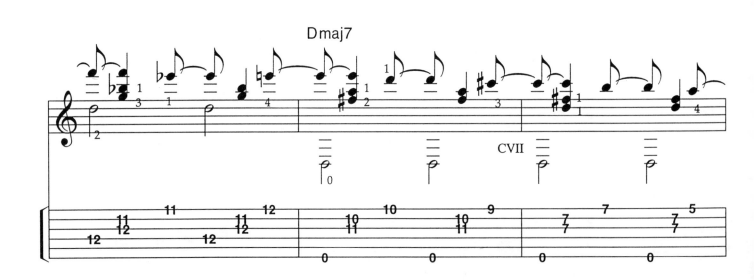

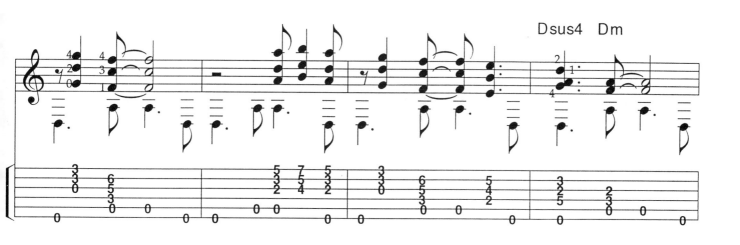

Jim Nichols

Jim Nichols has been a part of the jazz guitar scene for more than two decades, He has performed with artists such as Joe Pass, Toots Thielmans, Chet Atkins, Art Pepper, Julio Iglesias, Hubert Laws, Della Reese, Martin Taylor, Kenny Rankin and more.

Jim's music has taken him to the stages of Carnegie Hall, the Tonight Show and the Olympia theater in Paris. In 1997, Jim was a featured artist at the 18th annual Django Reinhardt Festival. Nichols' fingerstyle technique has earned him acclaim from many fans, as well as critics in the mainstream and music press.

Careless Love

Jim Nichols

Rubato

217

Jack Petersen

Jack Petersen has led a varied and successful career in the field of jazz performance and education. After attending the prestigious music school at North Texas State University, Petersen served in the 8th Army Band, and later toured with Hal MacIntyre. Other performances included dates with the Dallas and Fort Worth Symphonies, as well as Stan Kenton, Doc Severinsen, Art Van Damme, Joe Morello, Billy Daniels, Johnny Smith, Howard Roberts, Nancy Wilson, Clark Terry, Phil Wilson, Carl Fontanta, Rich Matteson and many others, and Petersen is also a featured member of the Matteson-Phillips Tuba Jazz Consort.

As an educator, Petersen served as head of the guitar department at the Berklee College of Music in Boston for three years. He was also on the faculties of the Stan Kenton Clinics, the National Stage Band Clinics, Jamey Aebersold Combo Camps, Clark Terry Summer Jazz Camp and the Rich Matteson Summer Jazz Camp. Petersen was a faculty member of the Summer Music Camps in Sweden for three years. Petersen served as Resident Artist for 12 years at North Texas State University while serving as a teacher of guitar, improvisation and lab band. Petersen was Resident Artist/Associate Professor teaching guitar, improvisation, and Jazz Ensemble at the University of North Florida School of Music in Jacksonville, Florida.

Petersen is the author of two texts on improvisation, and is a staff artist/clinician for Fender amps and guitars. He currently resides and performs in Sarasota, Florida.

Groovey!
(Melody)

Jack Petersen

223

Groovey!
(Jazz Solo)

Jack Petersen

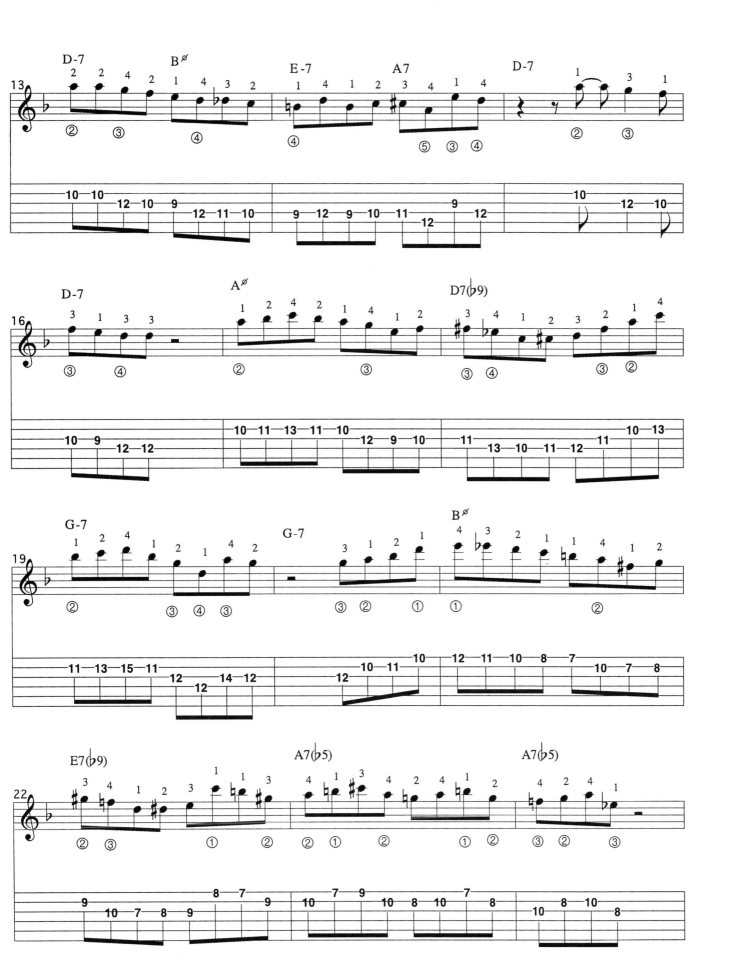

225

Bill Piburn

Bill Piburn is a native of Kansas City, Missouri and now resides in Nashville, Tennessee. He studied classical guitar with Douglas Niedl and Christopher Parkening and studied jazz with pianist John Elliott. His transcriptions have appeared in *Acoustic Guitar Magazine* and he has been a columnist for *Fingerstyle Guitar* and *Just Jazz Guitar* magazines. He is the author of *Mel Bay's Complete Book of Fiddle Tunes for Acoustic Guitar* (95471).

Bill's playing and arranging have won him praise from guitarist such as Martin Taylor, Charlie Byrd, Joge Morel, Chet Atkins and Jack Wilkins.

Prince John

Bill Piburn

Even Eighth's

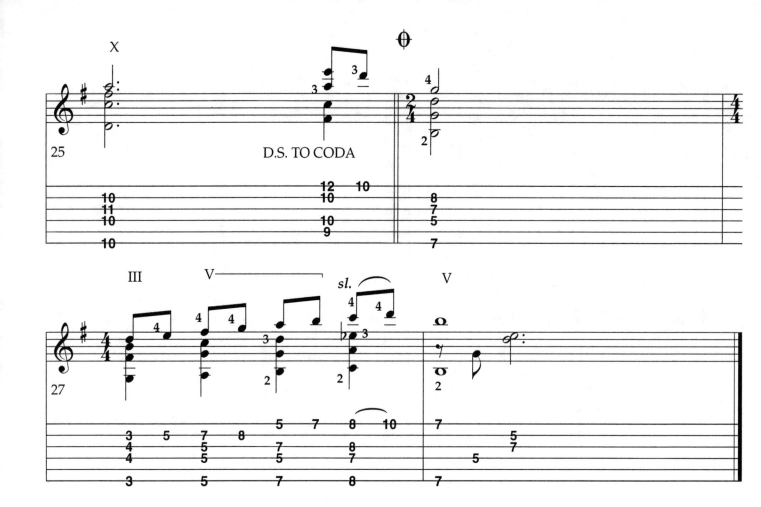

John "Bucky" Pizzarelli

John "Bucky" Pizzarelli is an internationally renowned man of music. His instrument of choice is the guitar, and his style is jazz. For more that half a century, "Bucky," as he is affectionately known, has been a part of the fraternity of musicians who have kept mainstream and traditional jazz alive. The list of big bands and vocalists with whom Bucky has performed and recorded reads like a veritable *Who's Who of Jazz*. He joined Vaughn Monroe's band while still in high school and later played with studio bands at the major networks. There he distinguished himself as one of the best rhythm guitarists in the business. Not contented with studio work alone, he jammed with and accompanied the best in the pop and jazz world including George Barnes, Stéphane Grappellli, Slam Steward, Zoot Sims, Flip Phillips, and his sons Martin and John Pizzarelli. Dedicated to swing and American popular song, Bucky is one of the most sought after guitarists in the business, and at a spry 72 years old, continues to enchant audiences worldwide.

Indy Annie

Bucky Pizzarelli

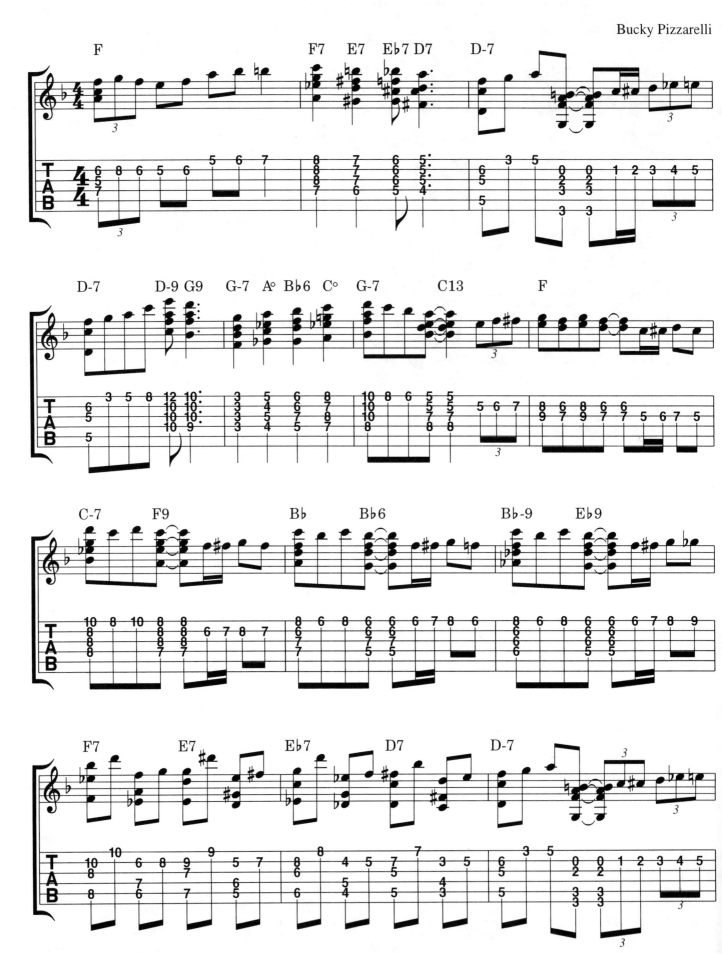

232

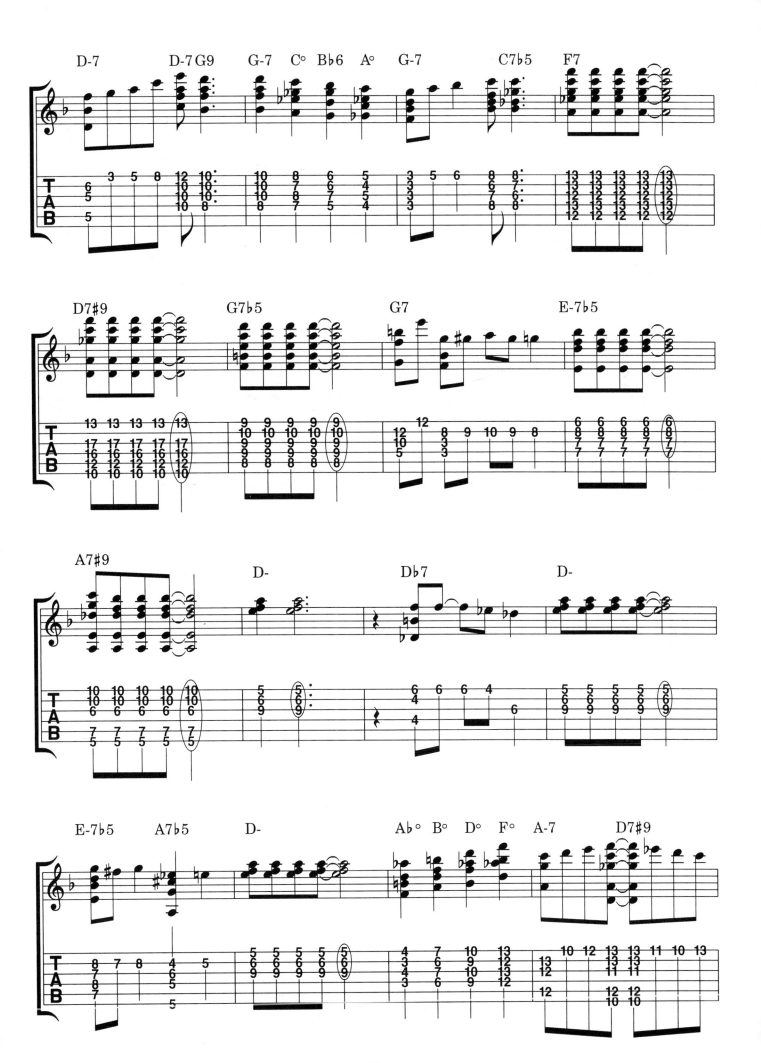

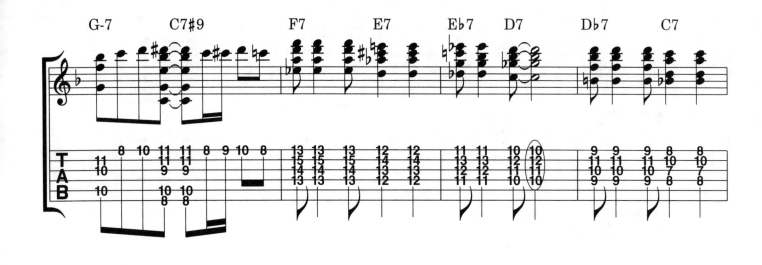

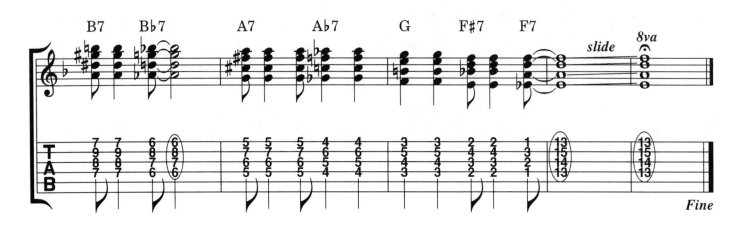

234

John Pizzarelli

John Pizzarelli has been playing guitar since age six, following in the tradition of his father, renowned jazz guitarist Bucky Pizzarelli. Hanging out with his father, John was exposed to all the great jazz music of the era, from Erroll Garner and Les Paul to Django Reinhardt. At 20, he began performing with his father. Then, he went out on his own, forming the trio with his brother Martin Pizzarelli, who had not played bass professionally before, and pianist Ray Kennedy, who has played with legends such as Nat Adderly, James Moody and Sonny Stitt as well as with Bucky Pizzarelli. It was Bucky who introduced Ray to John.

Since 1992, the John Pizzarelli Trio has toured Europe, the United States, Japan and South America extensively, even opening tour dates for Frank Sinatra and, along the way, they have earned rave reviews. Stehpen Holden wrote in the *New York Times* in 1999: "Like the Nat 'King' Cole Trio, Mr. Pizzarelli's trio balances a taut rhythmic intensity against an attitude of cool, intimate understatement."

For Pizzarelli, the comparison to the Nat "King" Cole Trio is the highest of compliments. "I've always said in my concerts that Nat 'King' Cole is why I do what I do. I was fortunate enough to meet (Cole's widow) Maria Cole, and she mentioned that when she saw us on television, she said, 'My God, it's the Trio.' I couldn't believe she said that to me." But, Pizzarelli quickly adds, "We aren't trying to copy him. That sound was so singular and inspired. I've always said we're an extension, a '90s version of what that group was."

John Pizzarelli has built a winning career on classic standards and late-night ballads and his highly-regarded guitar work, creating a sound and an atmosphere that have won over a new audience ready to swing and swoon. Using greats like Nat "King" Cole and Frank Sinatra and the songs of writers like Sammy Cahn, George and Ira Gershwin, Johnny Mercer and Jimmy Van Heusen as touchstones, Pizzarelli is among the prime interpreters of the popular American songbook, bringing to his work the cool jazz flavor of his brilliant guitar playing, and investing the eloquence of these masters with a contemporary flavor.

Ep's Frets

*Note—seven string arrangement. ⑦ =A

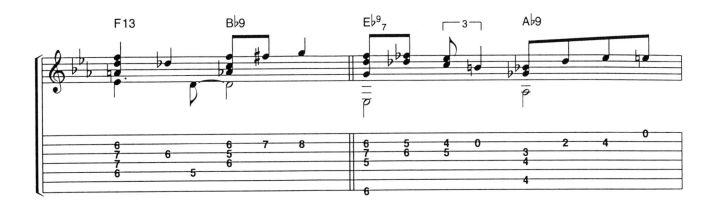

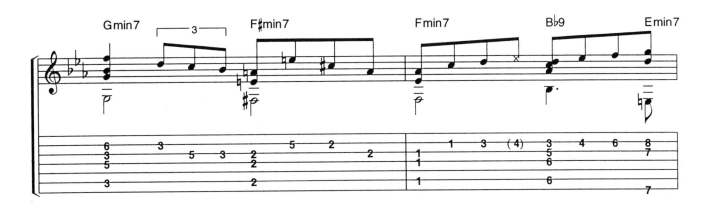

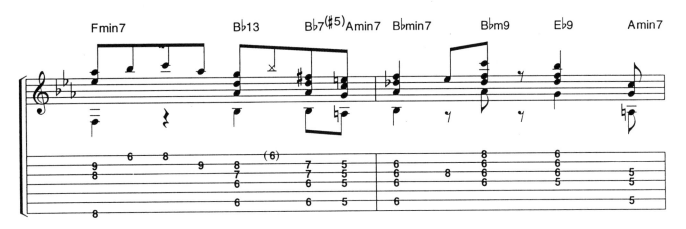

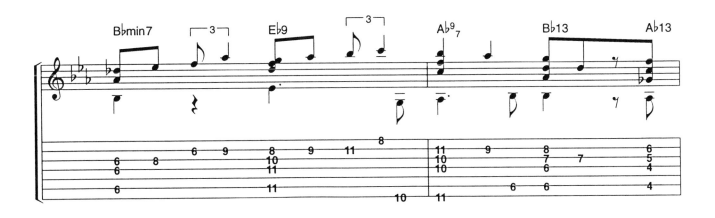

237

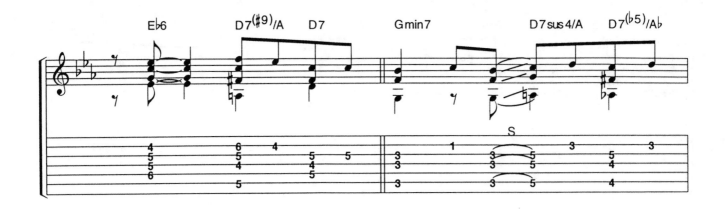

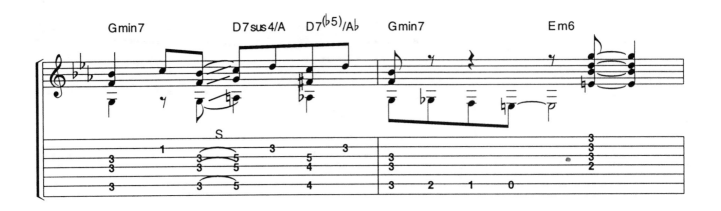

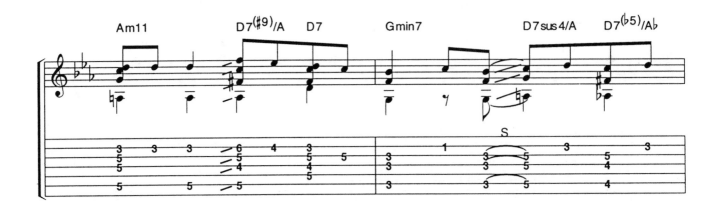

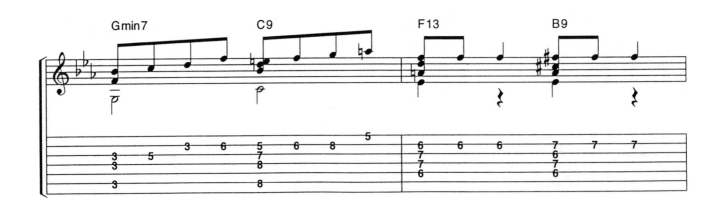

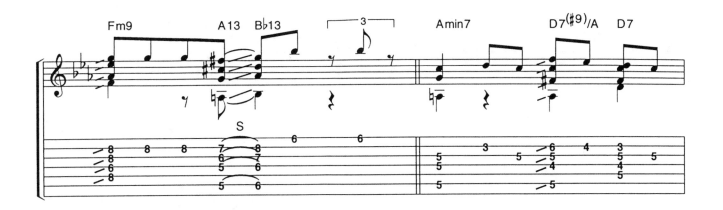

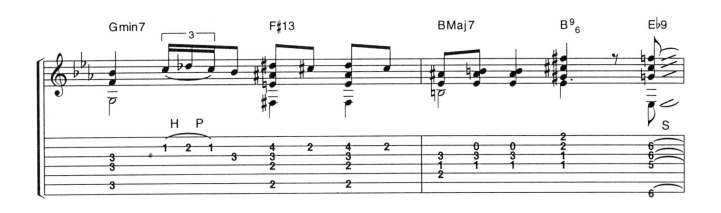

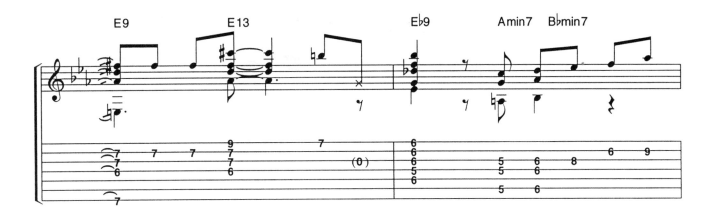

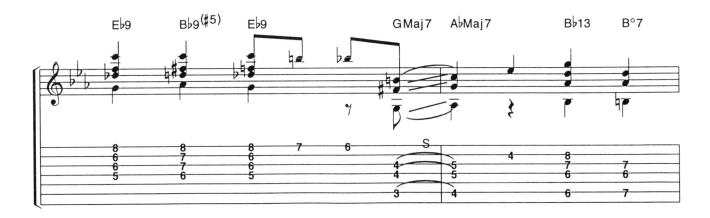

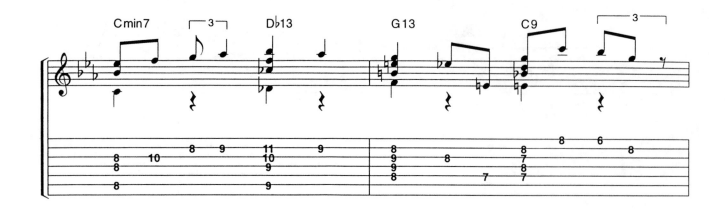

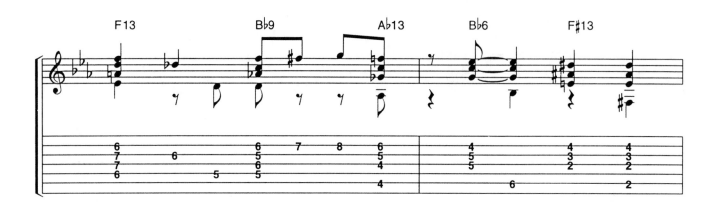

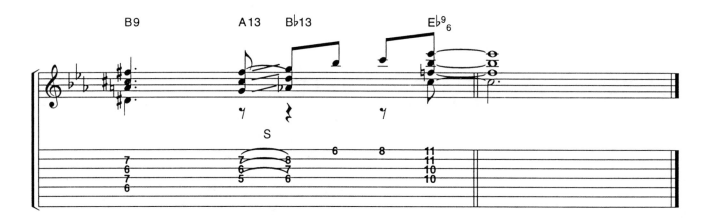

Joe Puma

Joe Puma has been a professional musician since 1948. He has performed and/or recorded with such jazz luminaries as Bill Evans, Herbie Mann, Cy Coleman, Louis Bellson, Artie Shaw, Kenny Clarke, Stan Getz, Lee Konitz, Jim Hall, Jimmy Raney, Tal Farlow, Ron Carter, Morgana King, Red Mitchell, Chuck Wayne and Oscar Pettiford among others. He continues to maintain a hectic performing schedule in the New York area.

BossAngo

Tempo Medium Bossa – Tango

Right Hand with Pick and Fingers

Joe Puma

244

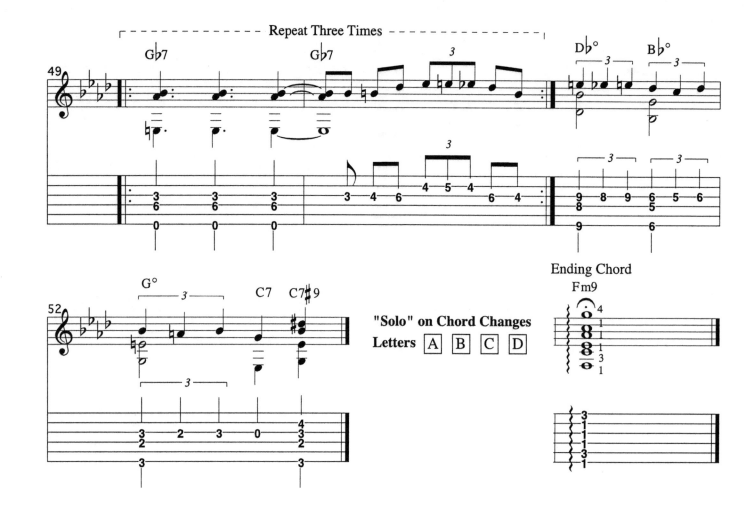

"Solo" on Chord Changes
Letters A B C D

Ending Chord
Fm9

Johnny Rector

Johnny Rector was born in Hickory, North Carolina and started playing guitar at the age of 13. He has been a free-lance guitarist/teacher in the Chicagoland area for the many years. Rector studied guitar under Joseph DePiano of Chicago, and he studied dance band arranging under the well-known Bill Russo of Chicago. Rector also studied a condensed Joseph Schillinger method under Daniel Garamoni also of Chicago.

He is the author of several well-known guitar books which have gained prominence throughout the country, and he is one of the most prolific writers of guitar material currently on the scene.

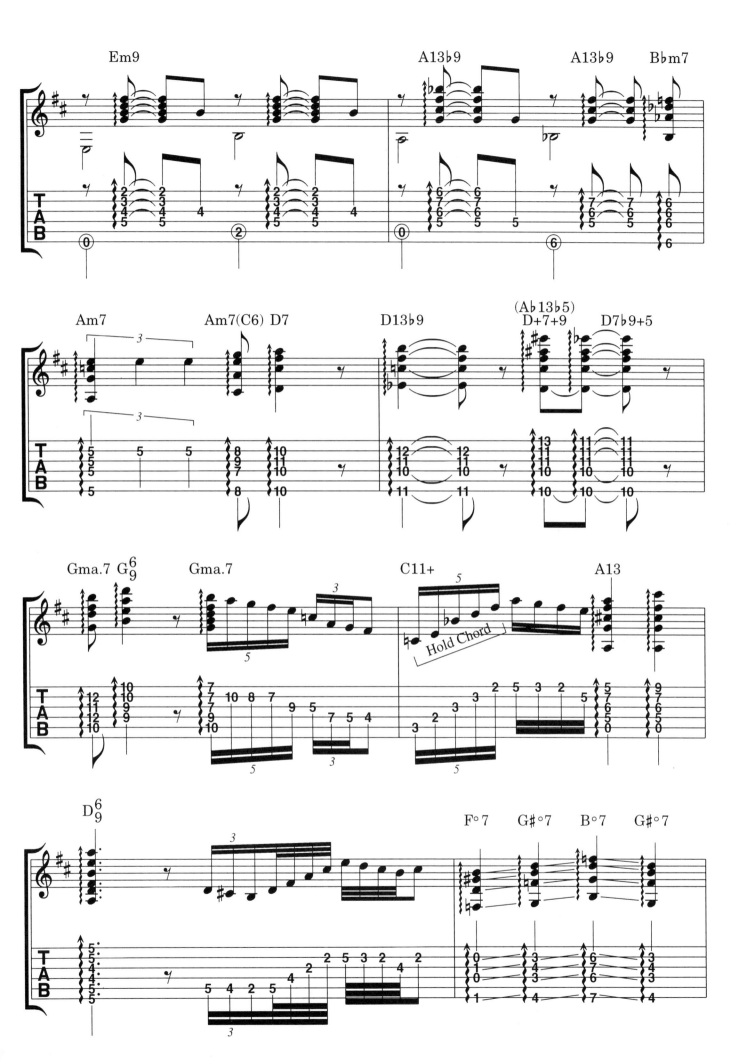

249

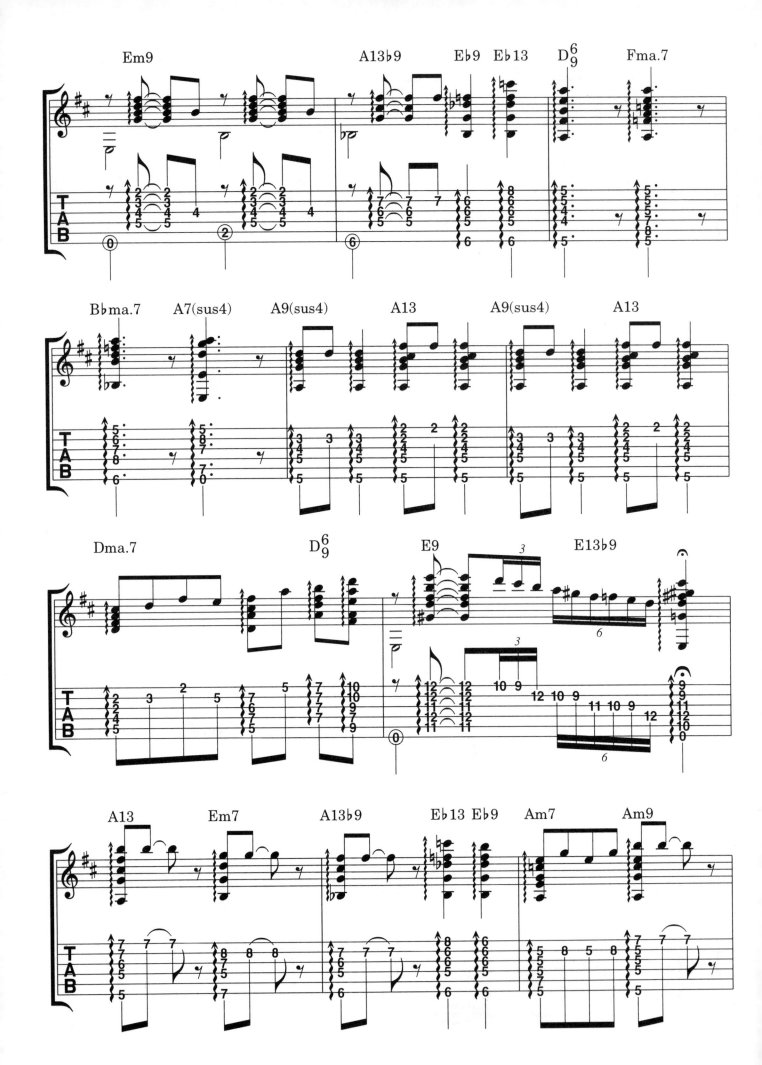

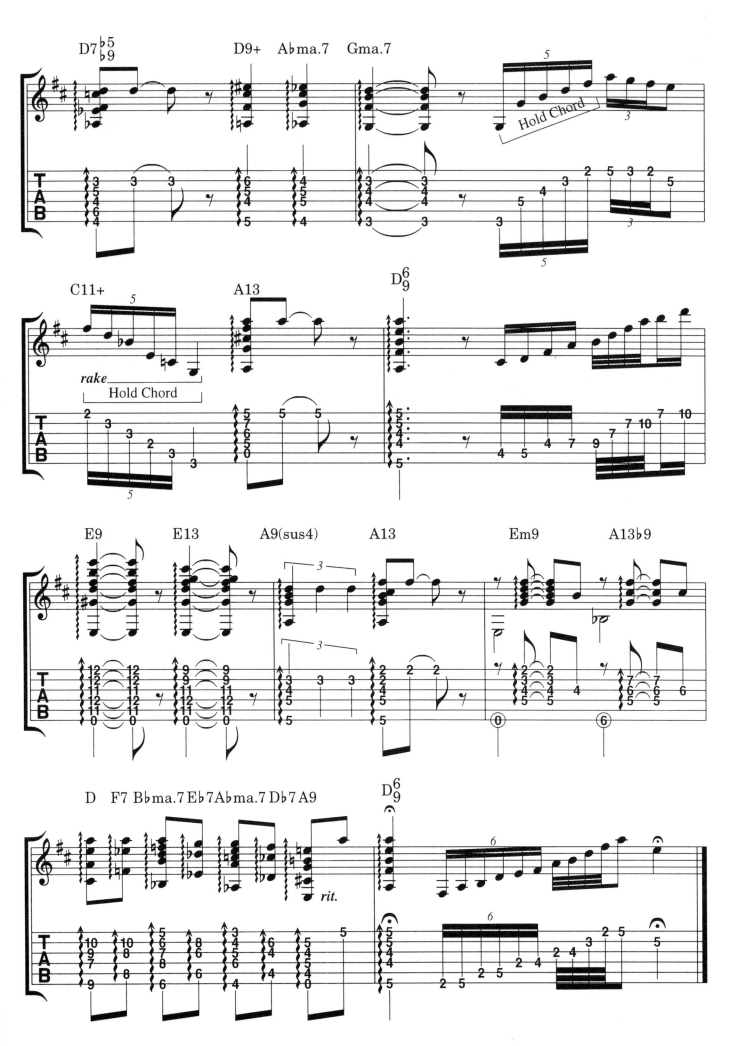

251

Sal Salvador

Sal Salvador was a self taught guitarist whose mastery of the jazz idiom earned him international acclaim. In 1945 Tommy Dorsey encouraged him to come to New York. Sal worked there with groups led by Mundell Lowe and Terry Gibbs. He landed a job at Radio City Music Hall and became a staff musician with Columbia Records. There he backed many of the legendary names in jazz such as Ella Fitzgerald, Sarah Vaughn and Tony Bennett. His roommates were Tal Farlow, Jimmy Raney and Phil Woods!

In 1952 Sal joined the Stan Kenton Orchestra and toured for 18 months. During this time he won acclaim for his renditions of such numbers as *Invention for Guitar and Trumpet* with Maynard Ferguson and *Frivolous Sal*. Next, he formed his own combo and was cited in the *Playboy* and *Downbeat* jazz polls. His composition, *Invention*, was used in the movie, *The Blackboard Jungle*. Sal recorded numerous albums for the Decca label, toured with Robert Goulet and Carol Lawrence and co-led a group for over a year with jazz drummer, Joe Morello. Sal was a devoted student of the jazz guitar and called legendary guitarist Johnny Smith his mentor. He wrote numerous books on jazz guitar technique, theory and improvising for Mel Bay Publications.

Campesina

Sal Salvador

Very freely

253

Zafar Saood

Born in Atlanta, Georgia on February 2, 1950, Zafar was christened Victor Herbert Vick, Jr. after American composer Victor Herbert. In 1991, he legally changed his name to Zafar Saalik Saood.

Zafar's family moved to Tuskegee, Alabama in 1957, where he began his musical studies—piano at age 7, clarinet and band lessons at age 9. At age 10, he taught himself ukulele and guitar after seeing Arthur Godfrey play uke and sing on his famed TV show and Bobby "Bobtail" Owens play guitar at a school assembly program. Zafar's lifelong interest in and proclivity for transcribing and arranging music was first apparent in elementary school when he provided scores for the various bands and vocal groups in which he participated.

Zafar and fellow classmate, Lionel Richie, played clarinet and piano together in several small groups. At age 16, Zafar was the first guitarist in a group known as "The Jays," which spawned the "Commodores." During the summers, he would return to Atlanta to study with his cousin and local jazz guitar icon, Wesley Jackson. With "Flat 5s and 9s," Zafar auditioned for Bill Braynon's Big Band. With Bill, he was allowed many solos and constantly was admonished simply to "Read wha's on the chart man!" Saxman Hank Moore had recruited Zafar for Bill's group (18 pieces), giving the teenager an opportunity to learn from "the cats."

In 1976, at Alabama State University, Zafar played with many virtuoso jazz players. When Aretha's sister, Erma Franklin, came to play in Montgomery, Zafar (then known as "Vic") headed out on the road as her guitarist and music director for several months in 1968. His mother did not even know where he was until a friend of hers saw him in Houston and reported him! With Erma's tour ending in Detroit, he was hired by Motown Records.

His absence from school came to the attention of the local draft board, and Zafar was shipped off to Kaiserlautern, Germany, where he played all over Europe. Zafar's group won five consecutive 1st prizes in all-Europe Talent Search, netting the grand prize of several tour dates which included affairs for NATO. Upon returning to the States, Zafar landed a major recording contract with Polydor Records. Unwilling to bow to the disco trend of the '70s, Zafar reentered school to study guitar.

After graduating from, Mercer University in 1979 (Psychology major/Music Composition minor), he went to Los Angeles and became co-writer with award-winning R&B songwriter/ producer Sam Dees. Zafar worked for "Knight Dees Knight Productions" (Sam Dees, Bubba and Gladys Knight) as writer and session musician/leader, and he recorded many dates for them. In 1980, Sam financed the release of an album *(Komputor Kid)* of Zafar's music, The title cut, *Video Jones*, was a smash hit with airplay and sales from New York City to Miami, and Zafar, as Komputor Kid, played coliseums and civic centers in the southeastern United States. In 1984, Zafar accompanied Michael Jackson on classical guitar while Michael wrote a song entitled *Lonely Man*.

In the Spring of 1994, Zafar competed for and won a full scholarship to Clayton State College to continue the study of the classical guitar. Zafar also studies clarinet, fluglehorn, and pocket trumpet.

(Capriccio No. 1, Opus 5)

Snowforest

Zafar Saalik Saood

♩=126

Legato

259

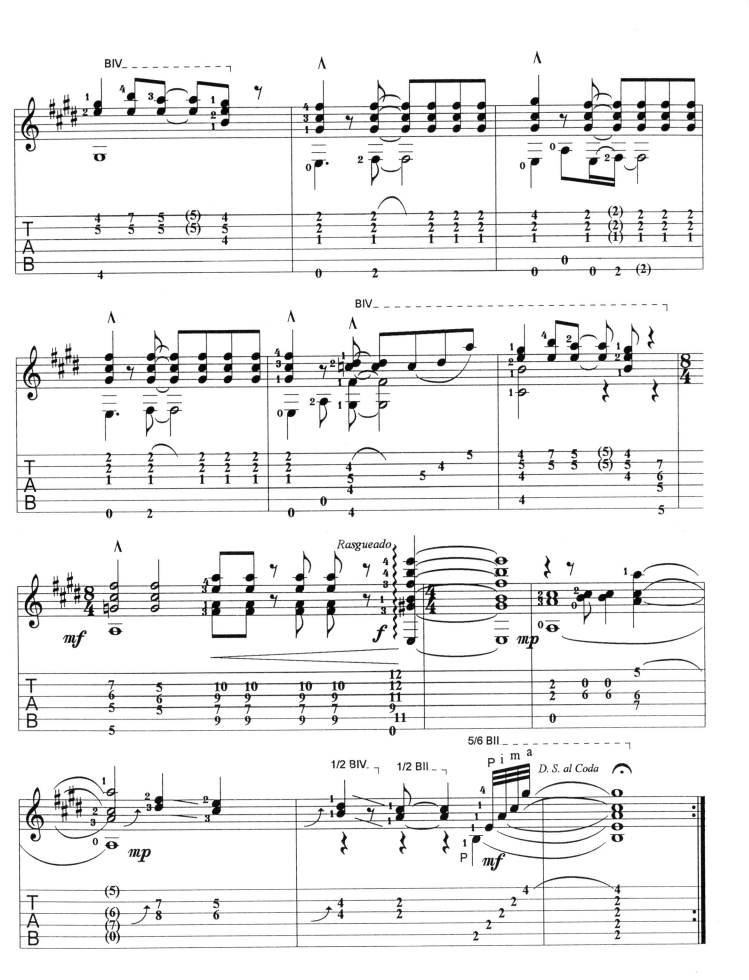

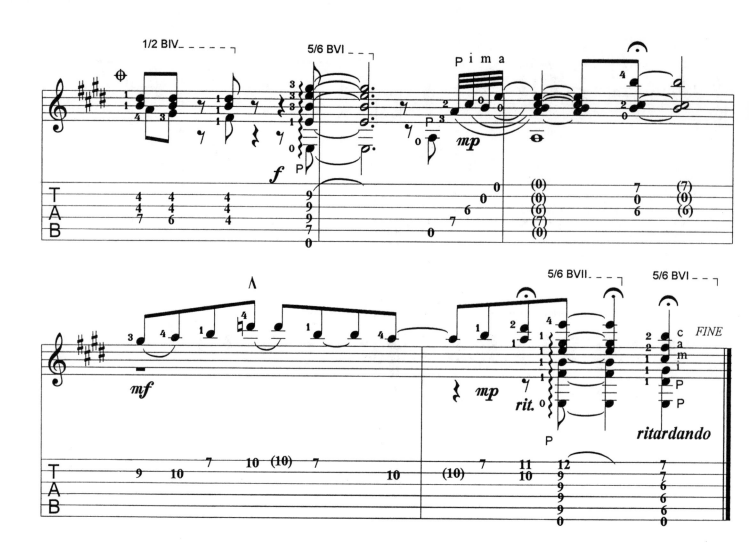

Jerry Sims

Playing guitar in a neighborhood band as a young boy was only the beginning for Jerry Sims. After graduating from high school in 1972 and touring with the Swingin' Medallions, a nationally recognized band of the late '60s and early '70s, Sims continued his love for his instrument by pursuing a musical education from Berklee College of Music. After graduating from Berklee in 1979, he moved back to South Carolina and opened Sims Music Inc., which has become a leading music retail and education center in the state. Sims has taught many students that have gone on to become successful musicians in the industry, including Mark Bryan of Hootie and the Blowfish.

After spending several years studying, teaching, and performing in Columbia, South Carolina on the six-string guitar, Sims heard Bucky Pizzarrelli playing a seven-string in 1982 and this was a new beginning for him. Sims made many trips to New York talking, listening, and getting advice from Bucky. Many transcriptions of Bucky's and Van Eps' arrangements paid off for Sims, and led him to be selected by the Ibanez Guitar Company in 1997 to represent their new 7-string jazz guitar. He was featured on their promotional video, *Seventh Heaven*, which also featured Steve Vai and John Petrucci. He was also selected to entertain at the NAMM music convention in Los Angeles, California.

Since being selected for this project by Bill Bay, Sims has been writing several 7-string guitar books to be published in the near future. A 7-string guitar solo CD is also in the works.

Just Like a Dream

This song was written and arranged on the seven-string guitar, with the seventh string tuned down to A, one octave below the fifth string. Although the song was written with the seven-string player in mind, all six string players should play it by moving the notes from the seventh string up to the fifth string. Hopefully each type of player will be pleased with the chord shapes that will be discovered.

Also, "Just Like a Dream" was written to be played finger-style. While learning this song you will see that sometimes as many as five notes are played at a time. I realize that some guitar players do not use all of the fingers on the right hand, but I think you will find it to be a great help if you practice this technique. If you would like to learn the song first without using your pinky, you may omit one of the notes inside of the chord. Usually the one next to the bass note.

During the composition and the arranging of this song, there were three main concerns that helped in its development:

1) To show the usage of the seventh string by creating bass lines and using chords that would include the seventh string.
2) Write a simple melody within a common song form that would be relatively easy to remember.
3) Use very common chord progressions that would allow the study of various ways to re-harmonize.

As you play this song, be sure to study and compare the first time through with the second time. I hope you will enjoy playing "Just Like a Dream" and learn as much as I did while arranging it. If you have any questions or comments, please feel free to email me at Sevenstrg1@aol.com.

263

Just Like a Dream

Music By: Jerry Sims
Arranged By: Jerry Sims

Guitar
7th string
tuned to A

264

David Smith

Jazz guitarist David Smith was born in Sydney, Australia, in 1954. He began his guitar study in 1973, and over the course of several years studied with Roy Plummer, George Golla, Ike Isaacs, and Joaquin Gomez. Smith began teaching private lessons in 1979. During his teaching career, he has given workshops and clinics for the Alambra Academy of Guitar, Mariah College, the Australian Guitar Institute, and NSW University. He has also held teaching positions at Panov Music Academy, the Australian Institute of Music, and NSW University. In 1998 he spent three months as Artist in Residence at the Conservatorium, Edith Cowan University, Perth.

Smith began performing with rock bands in 1973, and has played in solo and group settings in venues throughout the world. He has performed in clubs and hotels in London, New York, Spain, and throughout Australia. In 1998 he performed at the Manly, Kiama, and Cronulla Jazz Festivals. His solo recordings include *The Journey* and *My Funny Valentine*. Smith has also performed with New York guitarist Jack Wilkins on a duo CD *Alone Together* and on the debut CD of vocalist Kay Carter. His talent has been recognized by *Crescendo Jazz Magazine* (UK), the Jazz Guitar Society of Western Australia, *The Jazz Guitar* (UK), and *Just Jazz Guitar Magazine* (US).

June

David Smith

270

271

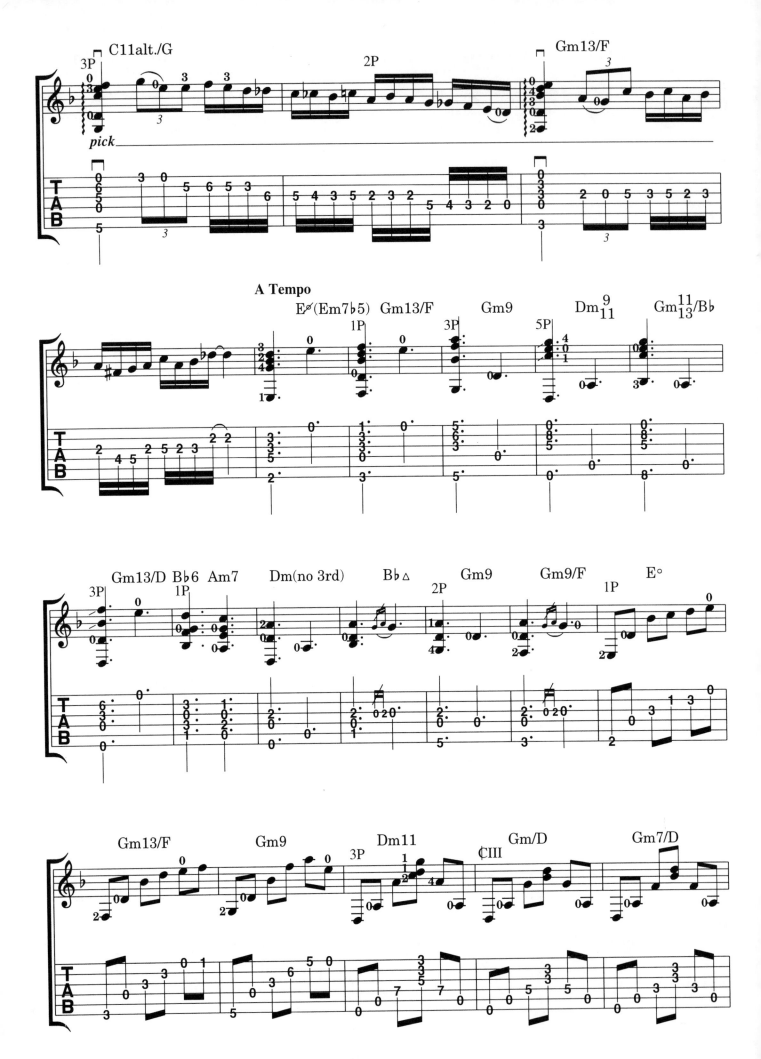

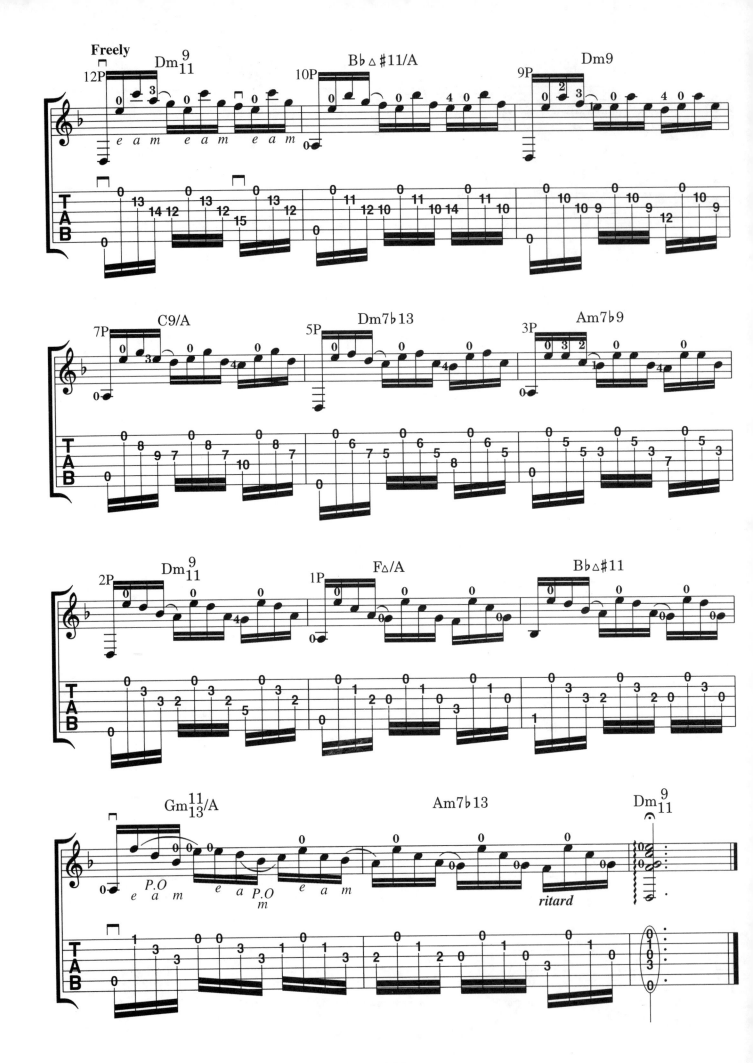

Johnny Smith

The guitar great Johnny Smith was honored June 15, 1999 by his peers in a tribute concert at the Kaye Playhouse in New York City. Over a dozen of the world's finest guitarists performed including Pat Martino, Mark Whitfield, Joe Puma, Howard Alden, John Abercrombie and Tony Mottola.

Smith, now at the age of 77, is considered to be one of the leading jazz guitarists of his generation. His soft-spoken and gentlemanly manner belie his breathtaking speed and agility, effortless chord work, melodic inventiveness and pleasing touch.

Johnny Smith, a self-taught guitarist greatly influenced by Andrés Segovia and Django Reinhardt came to prominence in the 1950s with his recording of *Moonlight in Vermont* featuring saxophonist Stan Getz. (*Downbeat's* readers voted *Moonlight in Vermont* one of the two best jazz records of 1952.) From 1947 to 1953, Smith was a staff guitarist at NBC's studio playing guitar and trumpet with both popular and symphonic groups, writing and performing for many shows, including The Fireside Theater and The Dave Garroway Show.

Aside from the dozen or more of his own recordings for Roost Records, Smith also recorded with Benny Goodman, Hank Jones, and Ray Brown. In the 1960s, Smith recorded an original composition *Walk Don't Run*, which the Ventures later transformed into an overnight rock and roll sensation. Striving for a better, unique guitar sound, Smith developed the Johnny Smith Guitar made by the Gibson Guitar Company. Since its introduction in 1960, it has been one of the most popular jazz archtop models.

In 1957, at the peak of his influence and popularity as a leader, Smith walked out of the limelight as suddenly as he had entered it, preferring the trout streams of the Colorado mountains than the night club stage. In fact, Smith says that "the most beautiful sight I ever saw was the New York skyline disappearing in my rearview mirror as I headed West."

Satan's Doll

By Johnny Smith
Arranged for Classical Guitar
and Recorded by Charles Postlewate

"With a Blues Feeling"

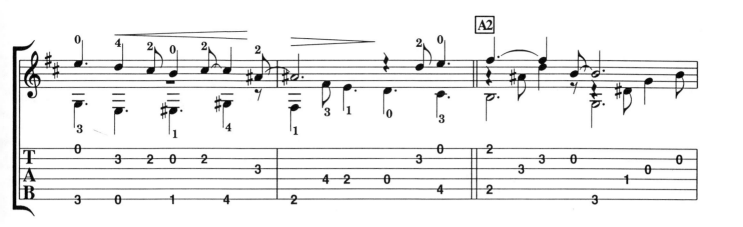

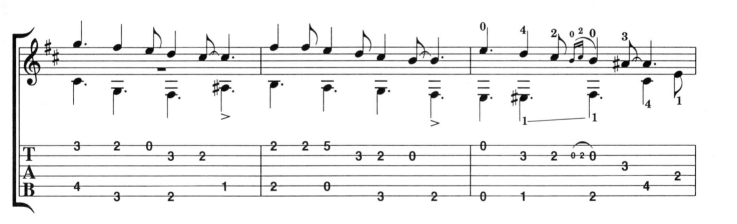

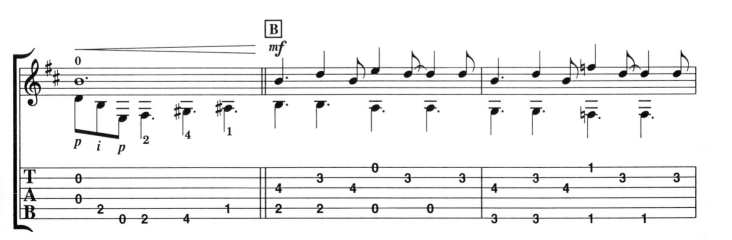

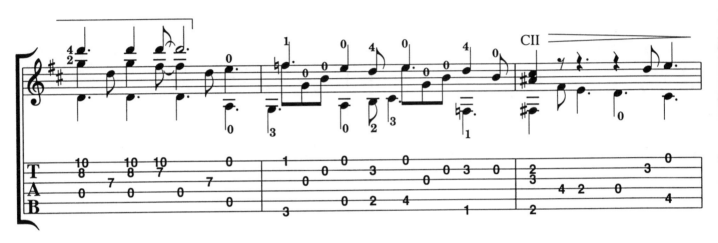

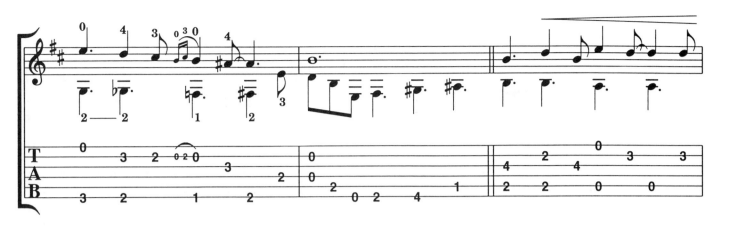

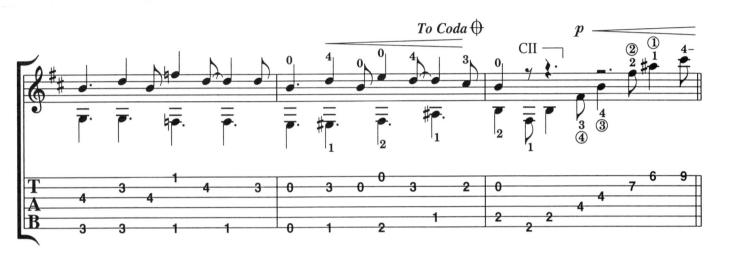

Improvisation

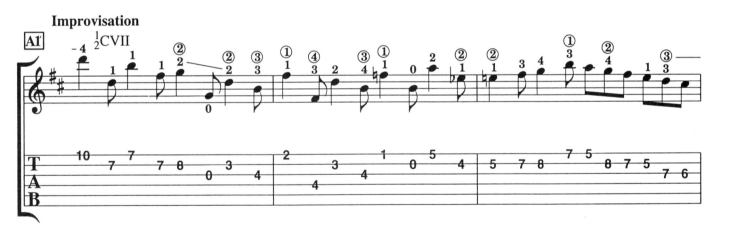

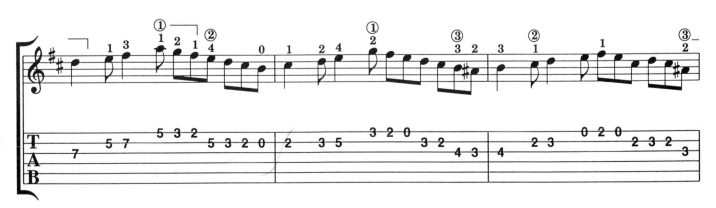

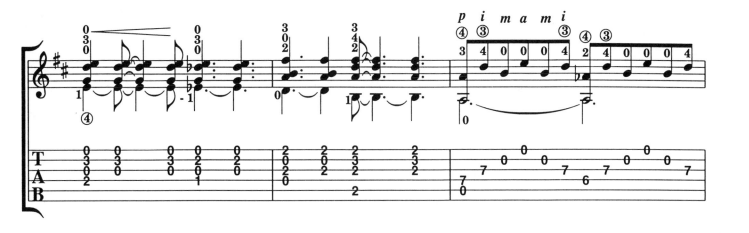

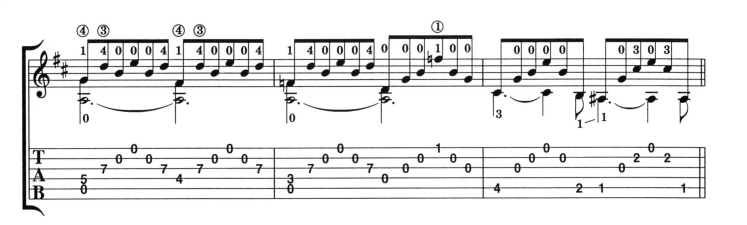

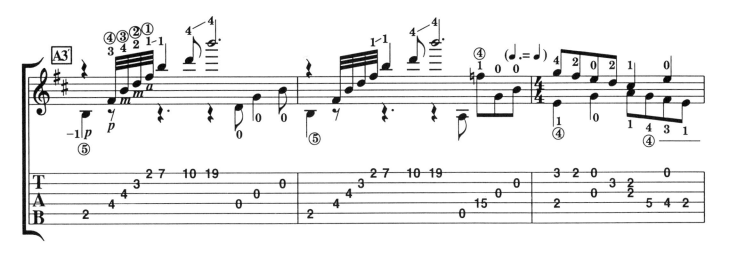

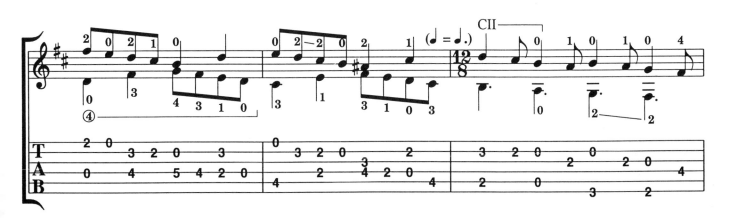

Lullaby

By Johnny Smith
Arranged for Classical Guitar
and Recorded by Charles Postlewate

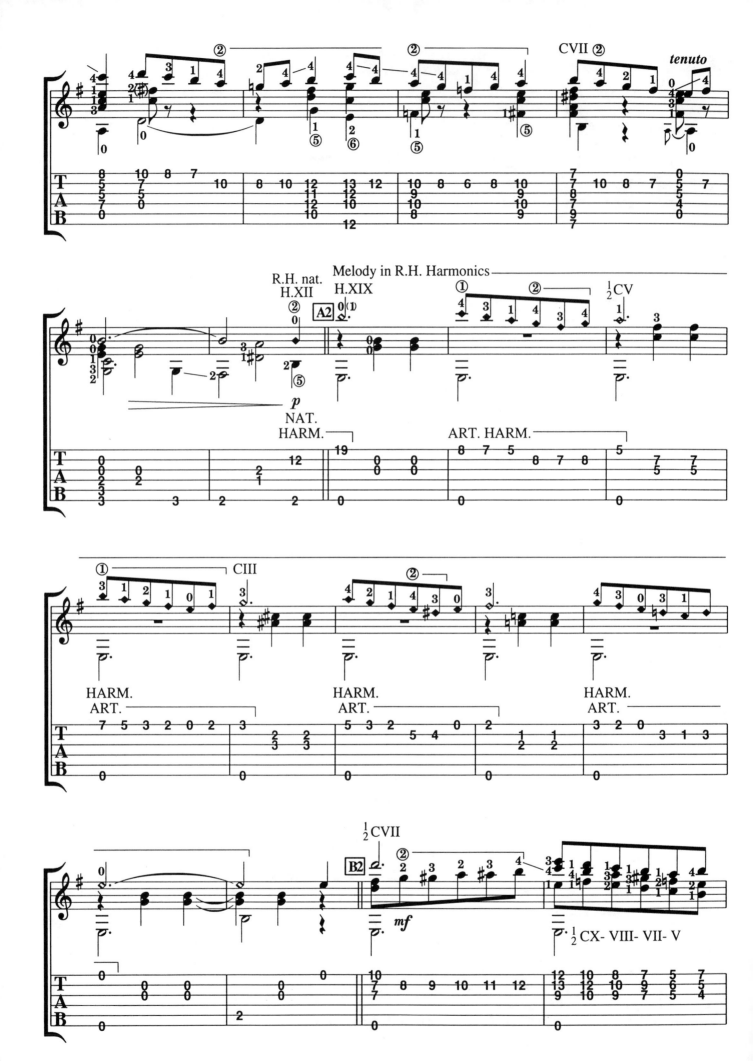

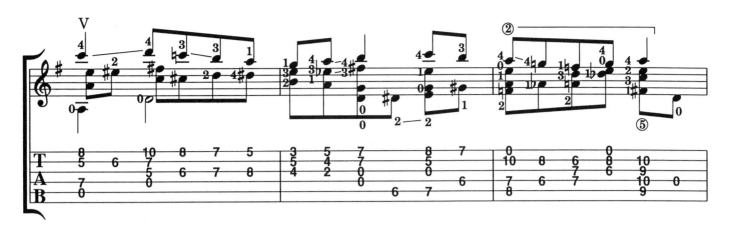

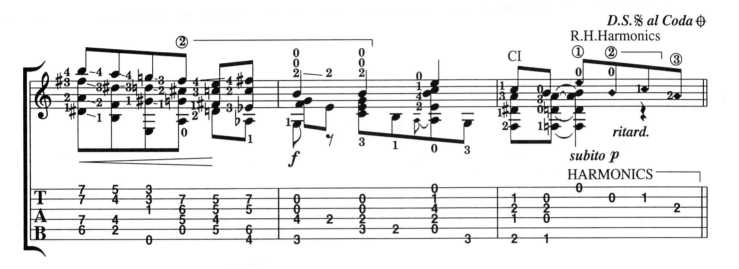

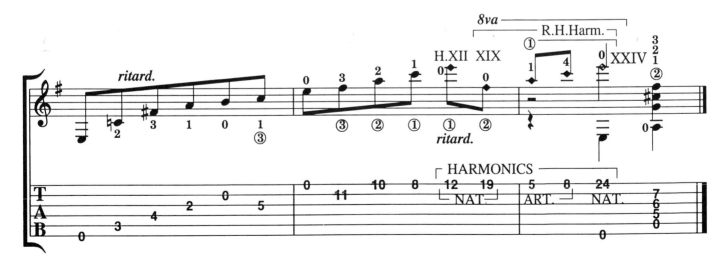

Fred Sokolow

Fred Sokolow is a versatile "musician's musician." A veteran jazz guitarist and singer, he is also an accomplished performer on the 5-string banjo, resonator guitar, and mandolin. Apart from his solo career, Fred has fronted his own jazz, bluegrass, and rock bands, and he has toured with notable performers such as Bobbie Gentry, Jim Stafford, and the Limeliters. In the recording studio, Sokolow has two recordings that showcase his talents. He has written more than 50 instructional guitar and banjo books, tapes and videos for seven major publishers. His books on jazz, rock, country and blues guitar styles are sold on six continents. Other guitar books and videos by Fred Sokolow include: *Beginner's Blues Guitar*-video (MB95208VX), *Best of Blues Guitar* (MB94138BCD), *Learn to Play Bottleneck Guitar* (MB94571BCD), and *Rockabilly Guitar* - video (MB95213VX).

Baby Brother

Fred Sokolow

287

Stanley Solow

Stanley Solow, instructor of guitar at Hofstra University, Hempstead, New York 1966-1986 and Nassau Community College, Garden City, New York 1970 to the present.

A resident of New York City, where he attended Public School 44 (Bronx); Dewitt Clinton High School, and Columbia University. Served in U.S. Army 1942-45 with 445 AAA Bn., 8th Inf. Div.

Married to Rescue Lady Freda; two loving children, Paula Nan (Mrs. Bruce) Watkins, and French hornist Harold Tobias, and their families.

Opus Untitled

Guitar

By: S. Solow

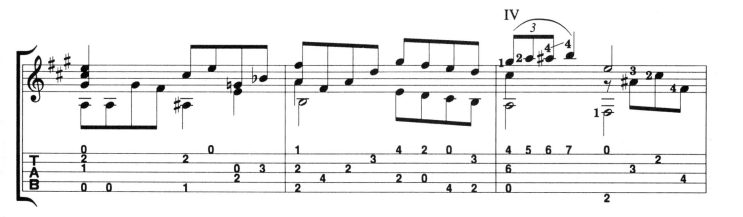

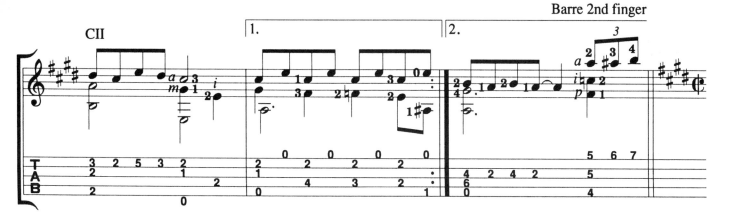

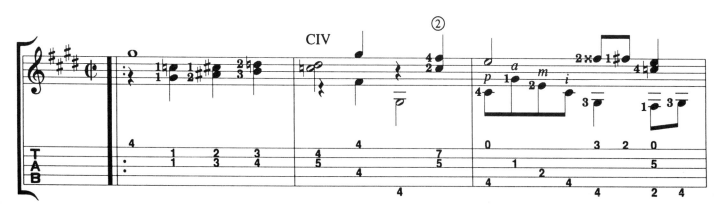

Chris Standring

Trained classically at the London College of Music, with ten years experience as a freelance session player in London, Chris headed for Los Angeles to put his artist career on the international map. He quickly integrated himself among the elite Hollywood music community enjoying success as a sideman both live and in the studio. Since his arrival in California he has recorded with Bebe & Cece Winans, Jodey Watley, Omar, The Solsonics, Carol Bayer Sager and Rick Braun. He has performed live with Marc Antoine, Rick Braun, Patti Austin, Bob James, Dave Koz, Richard Elliott, Boney James, Peter White, Kirk Whalum and Al Stewart.

In May 1996 Sonic Images records released his own acid jazz recording project *solarsystem*. The band was featured on the Stepping Stone 1995 compilation *Groovin' High*.

In February 1996, Chris took part in the "Guitar Saxes & More" US tour featuring Marc Antoine, Peter White, Kirk Whalum and Rick Braun. He then became part of Rick Braun's touring band for a year and a half and was featured as a writer and player on his top selling album *Body & Soul.*

The cutting edge New York based Instinct Records signed Chris to an exclusive artist deal in December of 1997. Chris has now launched his own solo recording career with a new hit album entitled *Velvet,* co-produced by *solarsystem* partner Rodney Lee. *Velvet* reached number nine on the Gavin and R & R radio charts peaking July 1998. Saxophone star Kirk Whalum guests on the record along with trumpeter Rick Braun. *Cool Shades* the radio single from *Velvet* went top 10 for over three months on the Gavin and R & R charts and stayed on the top 30 chart for 25 weeks! Chris' music has appeared on seven compilation CDs since his initial 1997 signing.

Recent headlining appearances have been *Taste of Orange County, Jazztrax Catalina Island Festival, Riverside Jazz Festival*, guest appearances with George Benson in Cincinatti and many more. Art Good this year pronounced Chris as the Debut Artist of the Year!

First of December

By Chris Standring

First of December

By Chris Standring

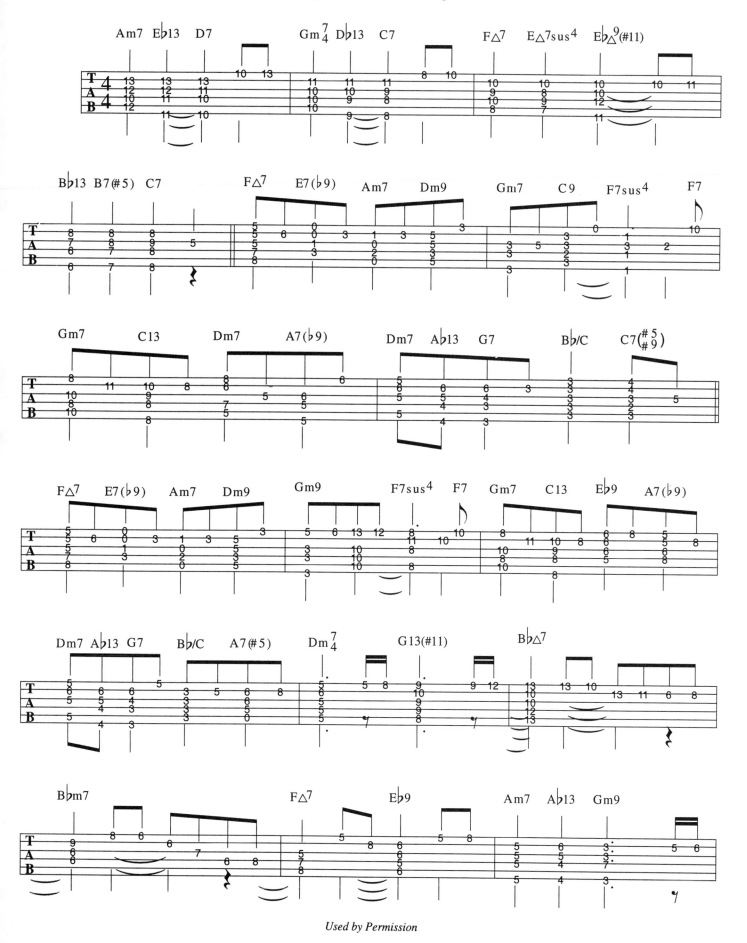

299

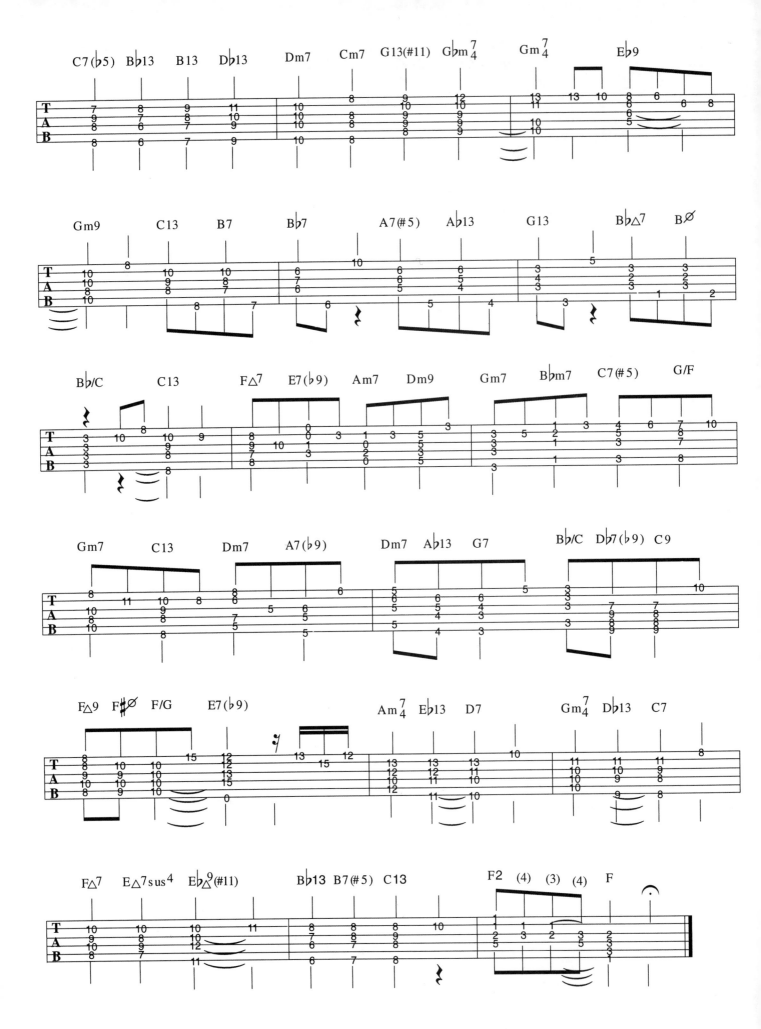

Jimmy Stewart

Photo by Dennis Trantham

Jimmy Stewart has played on more that 1,200 recordings with such legends as Quincy Jones, Ray Charles, Carlos Santana and Michael Jackson. He is a fast, tremendously facile guitarist who started guitar programs at Dick Grove School of Music and the Musicians Institute of Technology. He has written 27 books and received many jazz honors. On this recording of *Autumn Nocturne* Jimmy plays a vintage 1965 Johnny Smith Guitar.

Autumn Nocturne

by Jimmy Stewart

Andy Summers

Andy Summers is probably most widely known for his trenchant guitar work in with The Police in the early '80s. His playing from that period has left an indelible mark on guitarist's and music around the world.

Since the break-up of The Police in 1984, Andy has recorded eleven solo albums, scored several major films including *Down & Out In Beverly Hills* for Disney, (which was awarded "Best Film Soundtrack" by BMI), inbetween these projects he continues to tour the world regularly with his own group.

Currently recording for RCA Victor Andy lastest CD *Green Chimneys* is devoted to the music of Thelonius Monk.

Andy was inducted into the "Guitar Player Hall of Fame" after being voted number one guitarist for five consecutive years in *Guitar Player* magazine. He received a Grammy nomination for his solo album *The Golden Wire*. Since then, he has toured consistently throughout the world headlining regularly at festivals in Europe, South America & Japan including Montreux, Nice, North Sea, Montreal & Rio de Janeiro.

Evans Above

Andy Summers

305

308

Martin Taylor

Martin Taylor has been playing guitar for as long as he can remember, ever since his father gave him his first instrument at the age of four. It was to be the start of a career which has delighted audiences worldwide and drawn critical acclaim from some of the world's finest musicians.

He turned pro in 1964 at the age of eight—at least that's when his playing earned him a penny whistle from an appreciative music shop owner. By age eleven Taylor had his first electric guitar, a Guild Starfire, and he was listening intently to the recordings of pianists Bill Evans and Art Tatum as well as guitarists Barney Kessel, Kenny Burrell, and Wes Montgomery. He left school when he was fifteen, and has earned his living with a guitar ever since.

Chet Atkins, Barney Kessel, John Williams, Joe Pass, Stephane Grappelli, Toots Thielmans, Yehudi Menuhin, David Grisman, Steve Howe, Bill Wyman are just some of the musicians who have collaborated with Martin.

Anything Goes

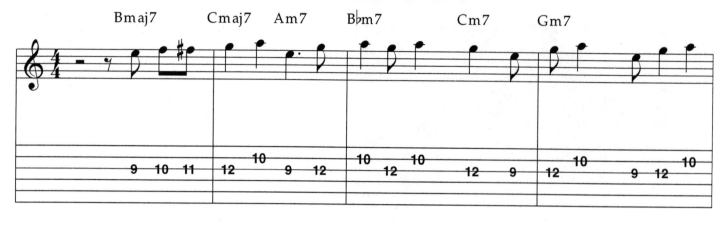

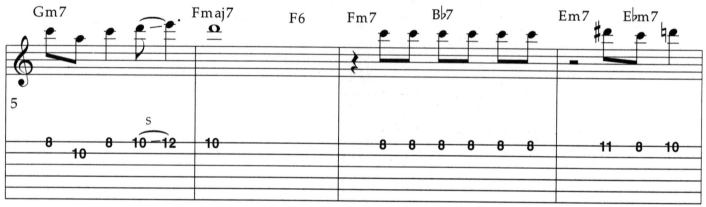

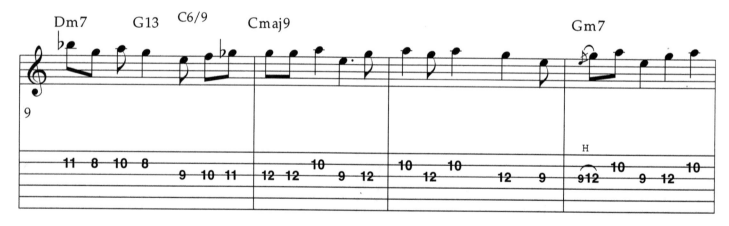

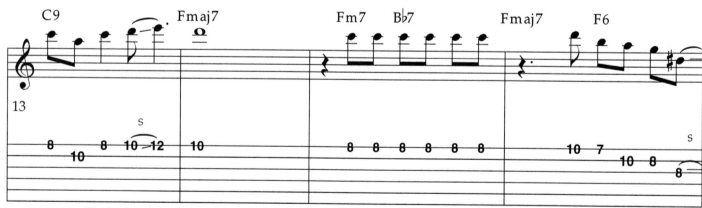

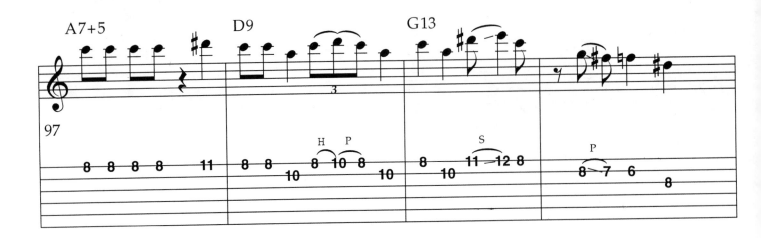

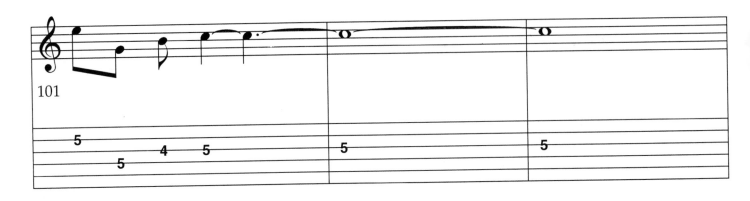

Jay Umble

Jay Umble has studied extensively with world-renowned guitarists Pat Martino and Joe Diorio, and has released two recordings which incorporate straight-ahead and modern jazz styles. He serves on the faculty of Bucknell University and Susquehanna University as a guitar instructor. He has several instructional books published through Mel Bay Publications that are endorsed by such jazz greats as Pat Martino, Joe Diorio, Steve Kahn, and Paul Bollenback. He has also written and recorded solo guitar pieces for the Anthology; *2000 Blues Guitar* (MB98424BCD) from Mel Bay Publications. He served as the jazz guitar clinician for the "Pennsylvania Mellon Jazz Festival." Jay also writes a monthly jazz guitar column for the *Central Pennsylvania Friends of Jazz* newsletter and performs regularly throughout Central Pennsylvania with his jazz trio and quartet.

Groovin' At Nick's

**SOLO GUITAR
(MEDIUM GROOVE)**

JAY UMBLE

Used by Permission

318

(D.S., take 2nd ending to Coda.)

Rit................................

Phil Upchurch

Born July 19, 1941, in Chicago, Phil Upchurch has been playing professionally since the age of 16 and began his recording career in 1958 at the age of 17 with people like Curtis Mayfield, Otis Rush, and Jimmy Reed.

Phil has gone on to play on thousands of commercials and albums for products and artists of every genre. He has recorded 16 albums of his own as a solo artist. He spent six years (1975-1981) touring and recording with George Benson.

George has recorded three of Phil's compositions. *6 to 4* was recorded on the multi platinum-selling album *Breezin'* and is to this day the largest-selling jazz album in history.

In 1985 Phil taught himself to read music through the study of Segovia's guitar transcriptions and has added MIDI guitar and computer technology to his wide repetoire of instruments. He is also a much-recorded bassist and has been sought out to play bass as well as guitar on the same sessiosn by many producers. One of the best examples of this is the title track from the album *Breezin'*.

Wes's Groove

Comp by Phil Upchurch

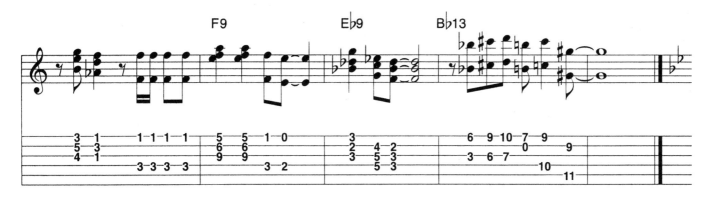

Used by Permission

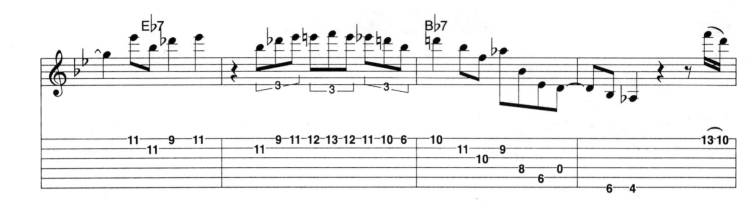

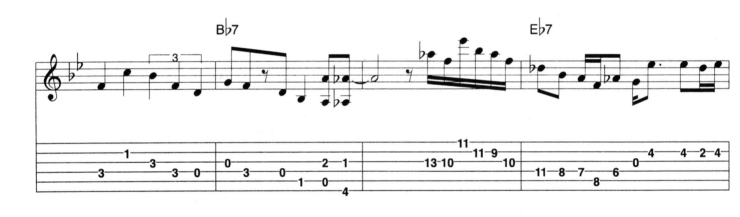

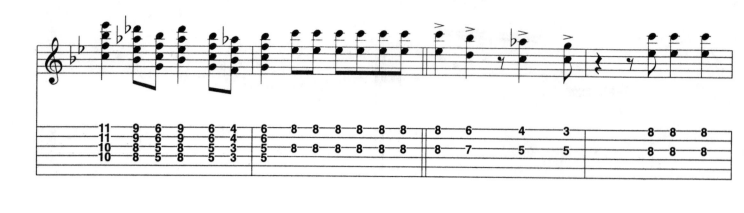

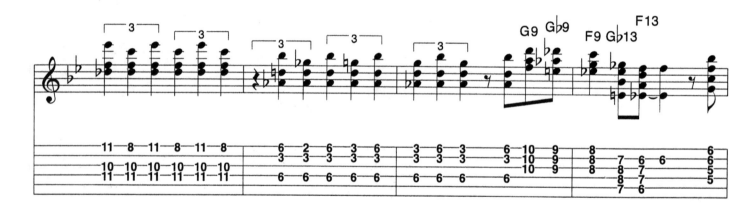

George Van Eps

Photo by John Crawford

George Van Eps was a legend on the guitar. His solos reflect his incredible knowledge of harmony as applied to the guitar fingerboard. In addition, his compositions transcend styles and eras. They are just as interesting, challenging, and valid today as when originally written. The solos lend themselves equally well to steel or nylon strings, electric or acoustic guitar.

Midnight

Lazy Slow Blues

GEORGE VAN EPS
copyist C. Chapman

(mm ♩ = 64)

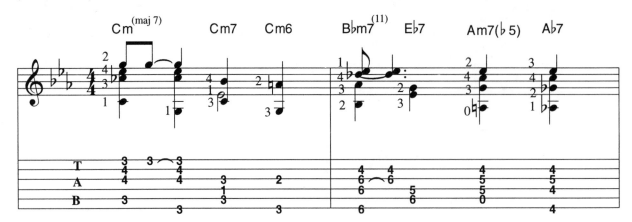

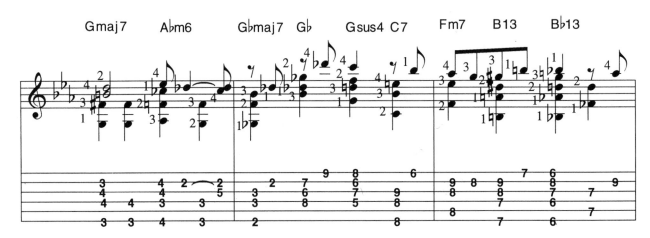

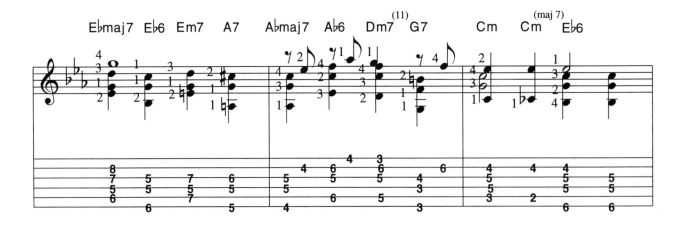

329

Squattin' At the Grotto

Recorded by Charles Chapman
BY JOHN AND GEORGE VAN EPS

Slow "2" Feel

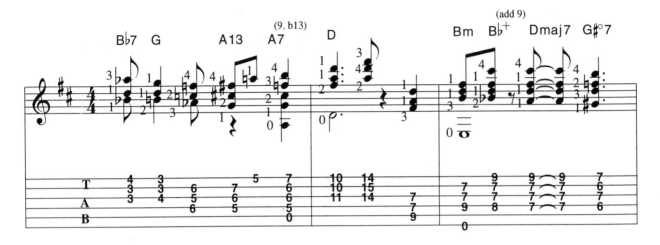

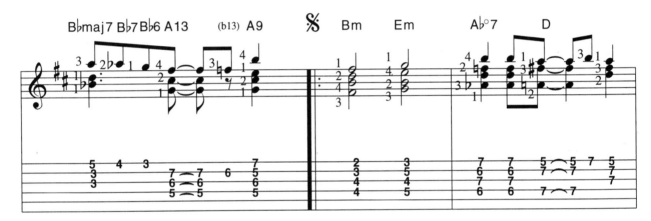

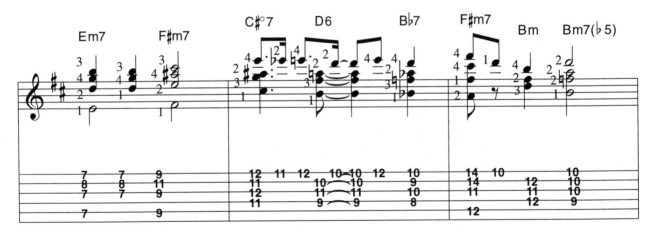

Used by Permission

332

333

Al Viola

Al Viola's Italian parentage provided him with a musical childhood in Brooklyn, New York. He learned to play all stringed instruments, then later concentrated on the guitar. Later came the formal training, followed by the professional work.

Viola's first job was in 1945 after being released from the Army. The group was called the Page Cavanaugh Trio, which made many tours throughout the United States, Europe and Canada as well as making recordings and movies. After that, he continued to work with some of the big bands such as Harry James, Ray Anthony, Les Brown and Nelson Riddle.

During the time that Viola was working with the big bands, he continued to study the classical guitar. His classical training paid off when he was asked to accompany and record with many artists such as Frank Sinatra, Peggy Lee, June Christie, Julie London, Steve Lawrence, Neil Diamond, David Clayton Thomas and Rod McKuen.

Viola first worked with Frank Sinatra in 1947 at the Waldorf Astoria Hotel in New York, then Atlantic Steel Pier after that. In 1962, he went on a world tour to raise funds for underprivileged children in each country where they performed. In 1973, Viola accompanied Sinatra at the White House when he performed there and continued to travel the world over again with him. Viola has done is television specials and most of his albums (the latest is *Trilogy*). Viola's other television credits include the *Hollywood Palace, Julie Andrews, Jonathon Winters, Don Knotts,* and *Andy Williams.*

His movie credits include, *West Side Story; Oklahoma; Who's Afraid of Virginia Wolf; The Godfather; Blazing Saddles* and many more. It was Viola's guitar that was heard on many TV commercials such as Viceroy, Budweiser, and many airline themes.

Viola's latest solo album is *Prelude to a Kiss* on the PBR label.

Sostenuto

Sostenuto: Sustaining the tone, giving notes full value. Played slow, some open notes like E♮, B♮, G♮, and A♮ add color to the prelude. Positions I to V and VII.

0—for open notes—as G, B, E, A, and D, when in front of note written. I, V etc. for fingerboard positions.

Sostenuto

Jack Wilkins

Guitarist Jack Wilkins has been a part of the New York jazz scene for more than four decades. His flawless technique and imaginative chordal approach have inspired collaborations with Chet Baker, Sarah Vaughan, Bob Brookmeyer, Buddy Rich and many others.

A native of Brooklyn Jack began playing guitar at age thirteen. His mentors included Johnny Smith, Django Reinhardt, Charlie Christian, Wes Montgomery, Joe Pass, Bill Evans, Clifford Brown and Freddie Hubbard.

Windows, his first album as a leader (Mainstream, 1973), has been critically acclaimed as a dazzling, seminal guitar trio work.

Later recordings, *Merge, Mexico, Call Him Reckless, Alien Army and Keep in Touch,* feature the Brecker Brothers, Eddie Gomez, Jack De Johnette, Al Foster, Phil Woods, Kenny Drew Jr., and many others. *Project G7*, a two CD set tribute to Wes Montgomery, features peerless chordal creativity by Wilkins.

In recent years, Wilkins has played at many international festivals and played with many jazz greats including Stanley Turrentine, Jimmy Heath, The Mingus Epitaph, 5 Guitars play Mingus (primary arranger) and bassist Eddie Gomez.

A consummate accompanist, Wilkins has played and recorded with renowned singers, Mel Tormé, Ray Charles, Morgana King, Sarah Vaughan, Tony Bennett, Manhattan Transfer, Nancy Marano and Jay Clayton. Wilkins was awarded an NEA grant in recognition of his work and contribution to the guitar. He has been widely and prominently profiled and featured in such publications as *Guitar Player, Just Jazz Guitar, Downbeat, 20th Century Guitar* and Leonard Feather's *Jazz Encyclopedia.*

Wilkins lives in Manhattan. He teaches at The New School and Manhattan School of Music. He was recently invited to judge the Monk Institute guitar competitions in Washington. He also conducts seminars and guitar clinics, both in New York and abroad. His latest CD, *Trioart*, on the Arabesque label, and a new video, *Jazz Guitar Workshop* (Bran Song Music), are currently available.

For Baden
From the CD "Trioart" (Arabesque Recordings AJ0135)

Bright Bossa

Intro ♩ = 108

By Jack Wilkins
Transcribed by Shane Simpson
and Paul Bourdeau

Fingerstyle

Used by Permission

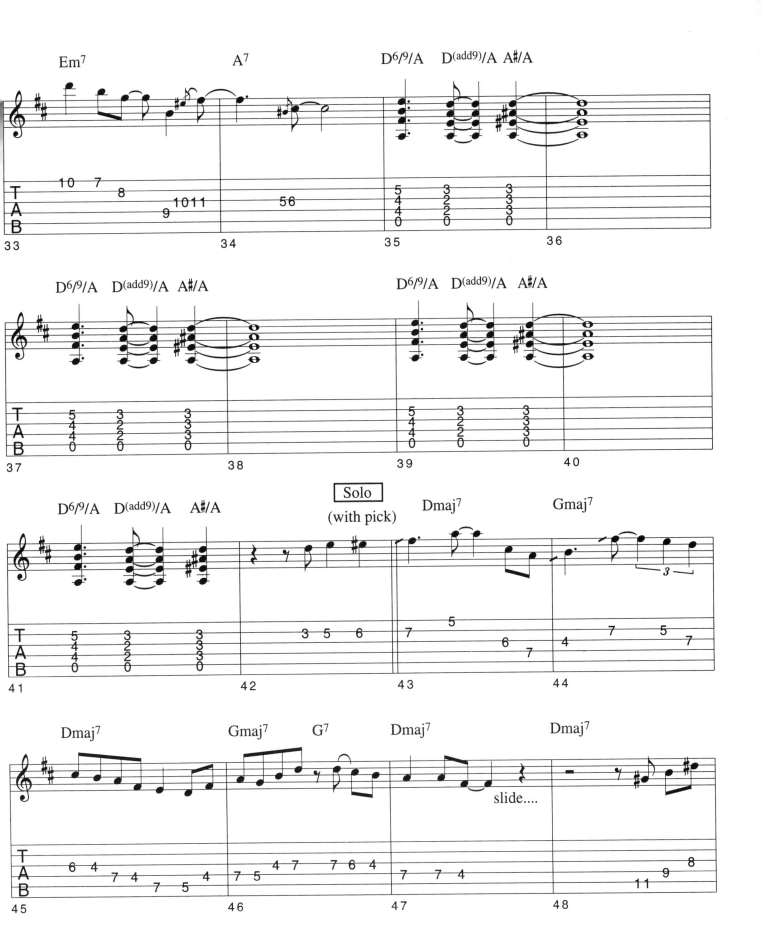

343

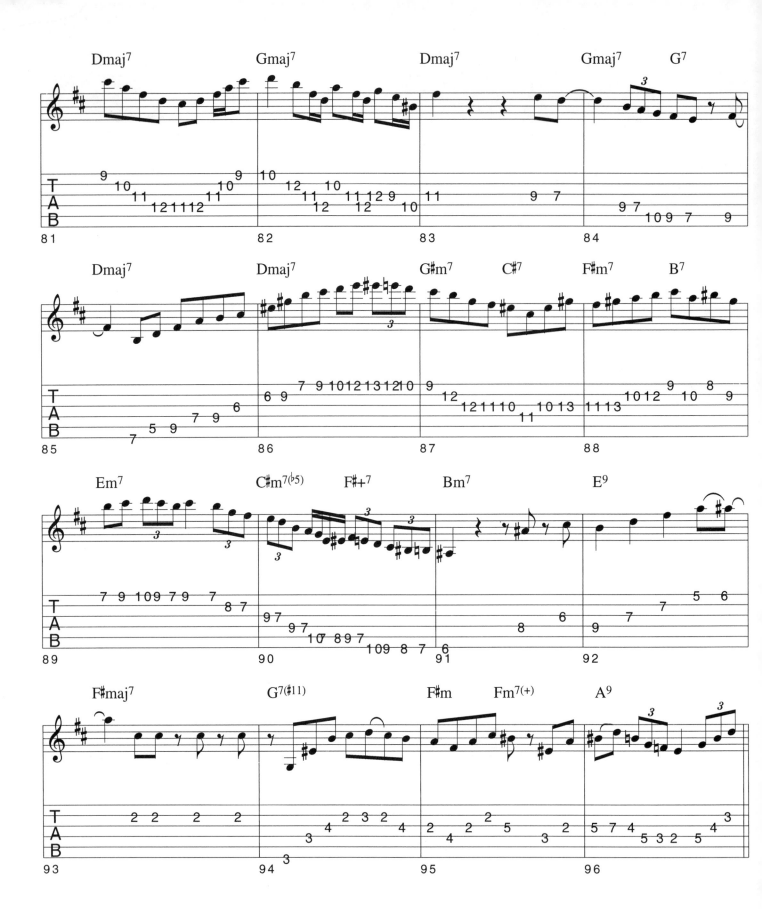

344

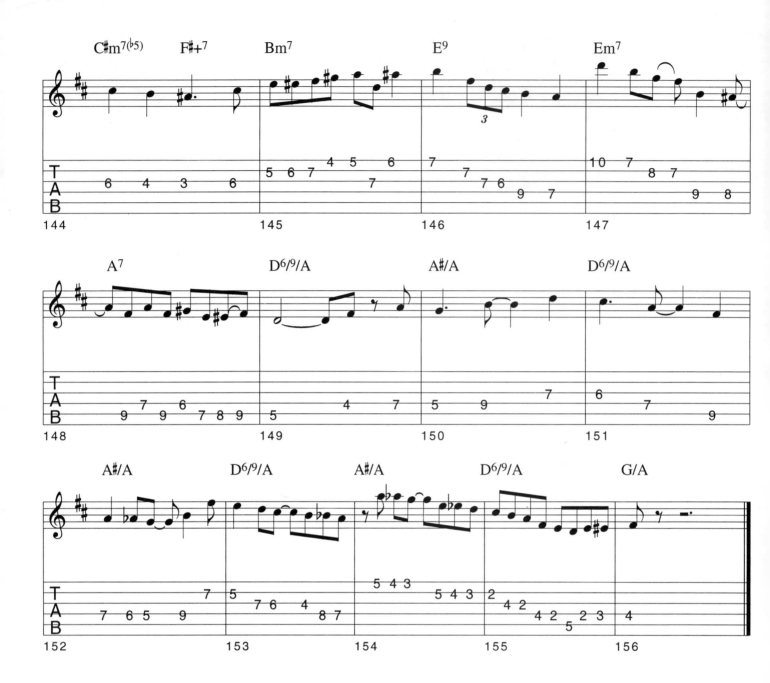

Stephen Wohlrab

Stephen Wohlrab is Associate Professor of Music at South Plains College in Levelland, Texas where he teaches jazz guitar, jazz combos and studio recording classes. He is a graduate of Berklee College of Music and also has a Masters of Music degree from the University of Miami. Stephen has performed with such nationally known artists as Sister Sledge, Jaco Pastorius and Carol Channing. He is currently very active in the Lubbock, Texas music scene and plays everything from jingles and musical theater productions to jazz and solo guitar gigs.

Pair of Fives

Steve Wohlrab

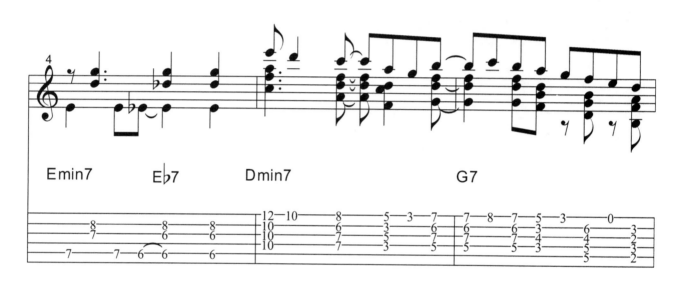

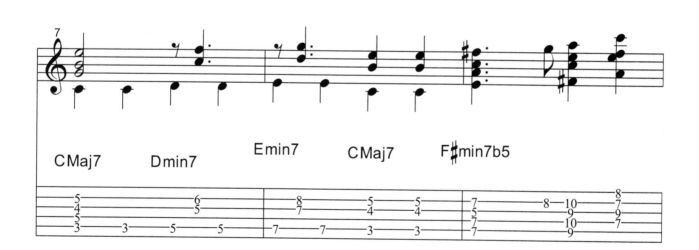

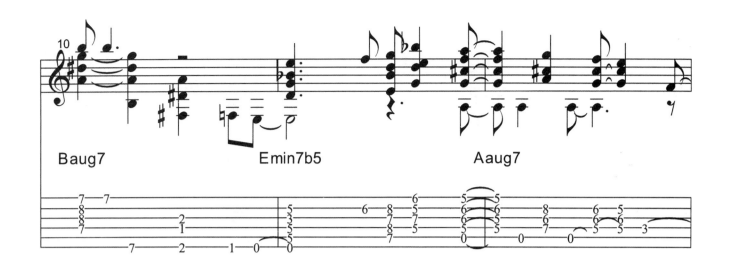

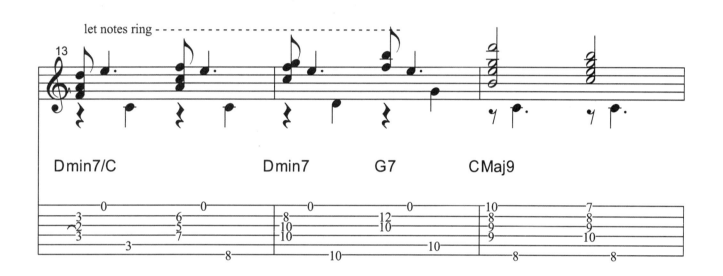

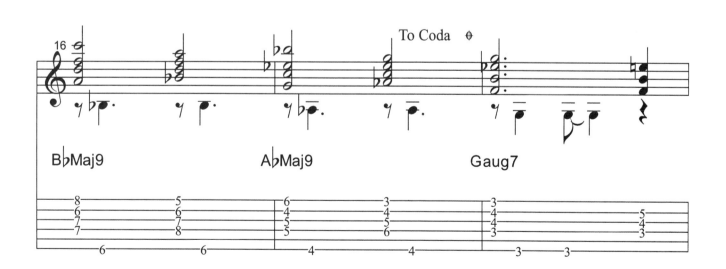

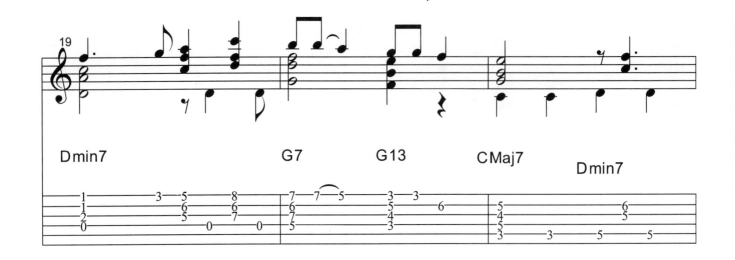

Dmin7   G7   G13   CMaj7

Dmin7

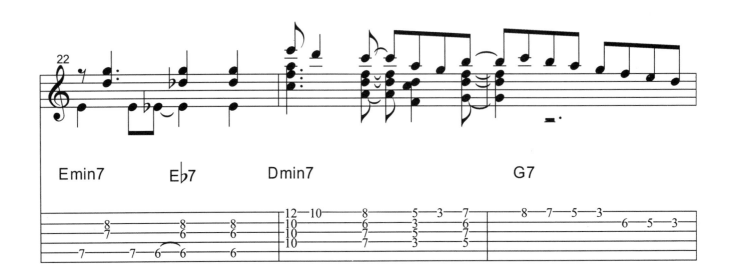

Emin7   E♭7   Dmin7   G7

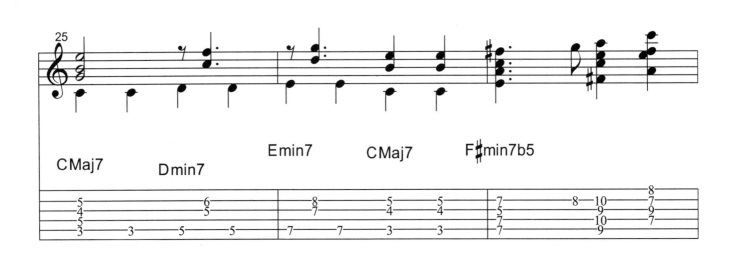

CMaj7   Dmin7   Emin7   CMaj7   F♯min7b5

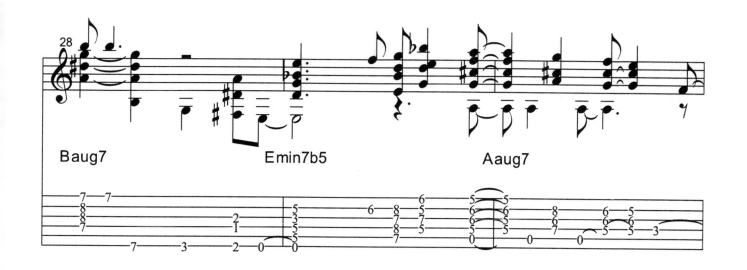

Baug7   Emin7b5   Aaug7

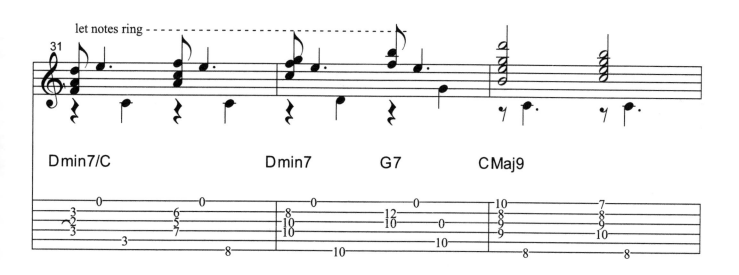

let notes ring -

Dmin7/C   Dmin7   G7   CMaj9

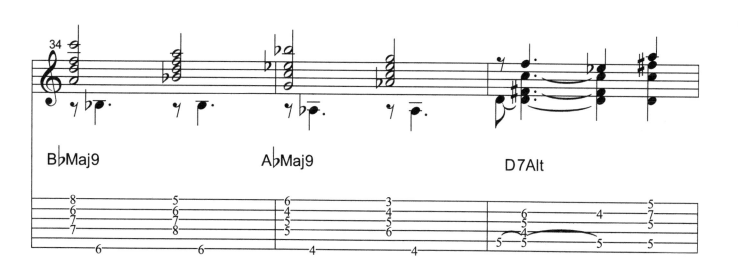

BbMaj9   AbMaj9   D7Alt

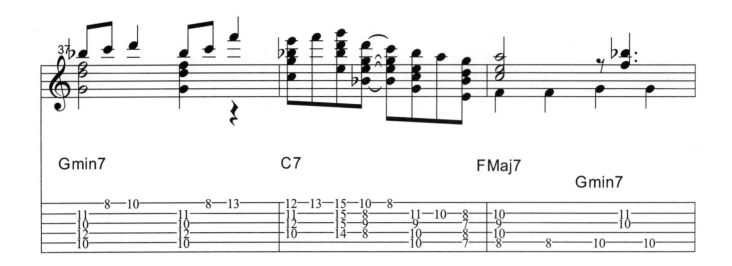

Gmin7

C7

FMaj7

Gmin7

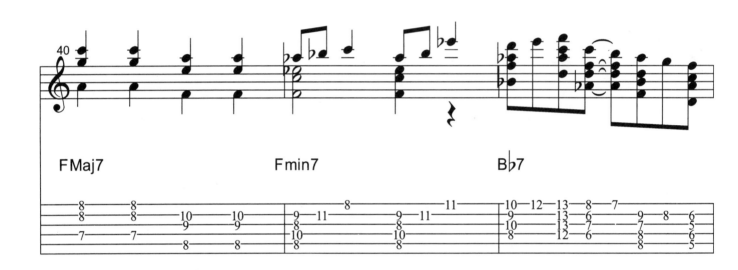

FMaj7

Fmin7

B♭7

E♭Maj7

Fmin7

E♭Maj7

E♭min7

A♭7   D7♭9   D♭Maj7

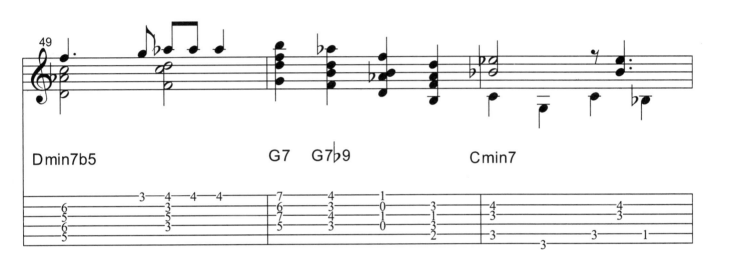

Dmin7b5   G7   G7♭9   Cmin7

D.C. al Coda

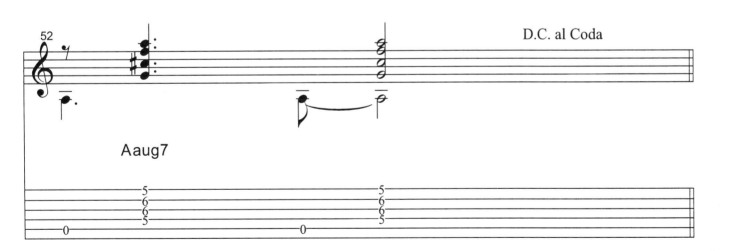

Aaug7

355

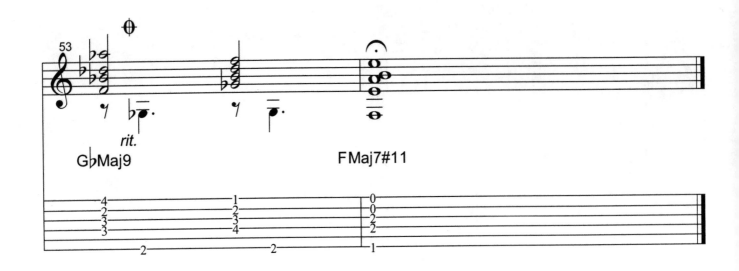

G♭Maj9 · rit.   FMaj7#11

Jimmy Wyble

Jimmy Wyble recorded with western swing bands led by Bob Wills and Spade Cooley, and played with the Sons of the Pioneers, Gene Autry, Lena Horne, Steve Lawrence and Eydie Gorme. His TV credits include: The Kraft Music Hall Specials, Phyllis Diller Show, Don Rickles and Andy Williams Shows and specials by Bing Crosby, Flip Wilson and Dick Clark. He spent nine years with Red Norvo's group, as well as filling the guitar chair in Benny Goodman's band and Frank Sinatra's traveling rhythm section. A studio guitarist from 1967 to 1983, Jimmy was a member of the famous *"Five Guitar"* group led by Tony Rizzi. His main guitar is a Roger Borys B120 that he has used since 1983.

Two Moods (for Lily)

Jimmy Wyble
edited by David Oakes

359

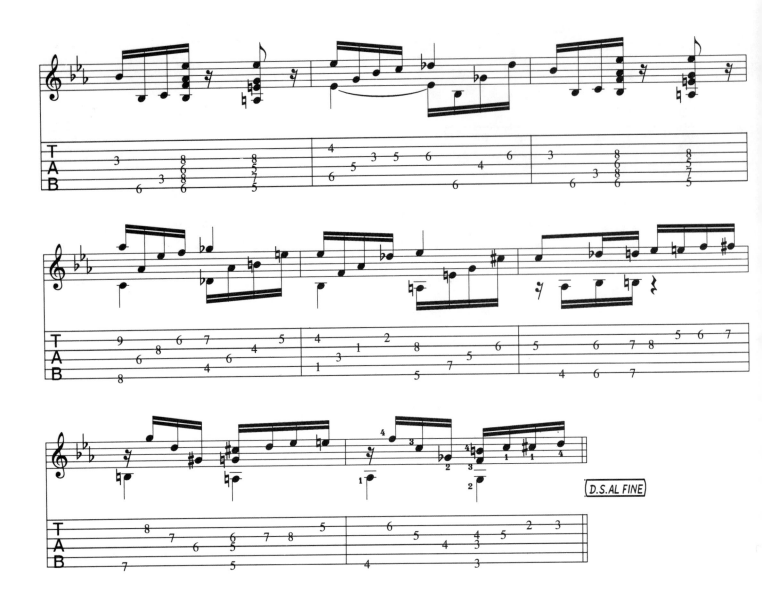

John Zaradin

Photo by Laurence Burns

John Zaradin is Europe's foremost player of classical Brazilian guitar music. His early training at the Royal College of Music and the Paris Conservatoire has combined with his deep involvement and love of the music and people of South America, to result in the unique sound he makes today.

John Zaradin holds a Gold Disc for his recording of the Rodrigo Concerto de Aranjuez on EMI's *Classics For Pleasure*, having sold over a quarter million copies. His other recordings of classical guitar music have included works by Vivaldi, Buxtehude, Cimarosa, Bach and Scarlatti.

After his formal training in London and Paris as a pupil of Alexander Lagoya, John Zaradin began composing and performing his own guitar music on both classical and Brazilian styles. His numerous works are currently published by Belwin-Mills and Hampton Guitar Music including the recent index of rhythm patterns - *A Unique Approach To The Study Of Rhythm*. John Zaradin has given live television and radio performances in the major musical centers of all five continents.

Over the years, John Zaradin has fused European formality with the spontaneity of Latin America, especially Brazil. His music has been played in concerts with John Dankworth, Paco Pena and other musicians. Brazilian music is now regarded as a valuable source of inspiration to contemporary composers in the same way that European folk music was to such composers as Bartok, Dvorak, and Brahms.

Faivo Klokti

Faivo Klokti is in 2 distinct parts, a 32 bar section in E minor & 2/4 time and an extended development in A minor with a basic 5/8 feel but some 6/8 changes as the music evolves.

Impovisation can be made over either or both sections, but i have found, in performing the piece that to ad lib over the 5/8 bars 34–41 and then use bars 42–76 as a solos ending (before returning to the first section as written) works well musically.

Faivo Klokti
Latin Fusion at Sharp 9 O'Clock

John Zaradin

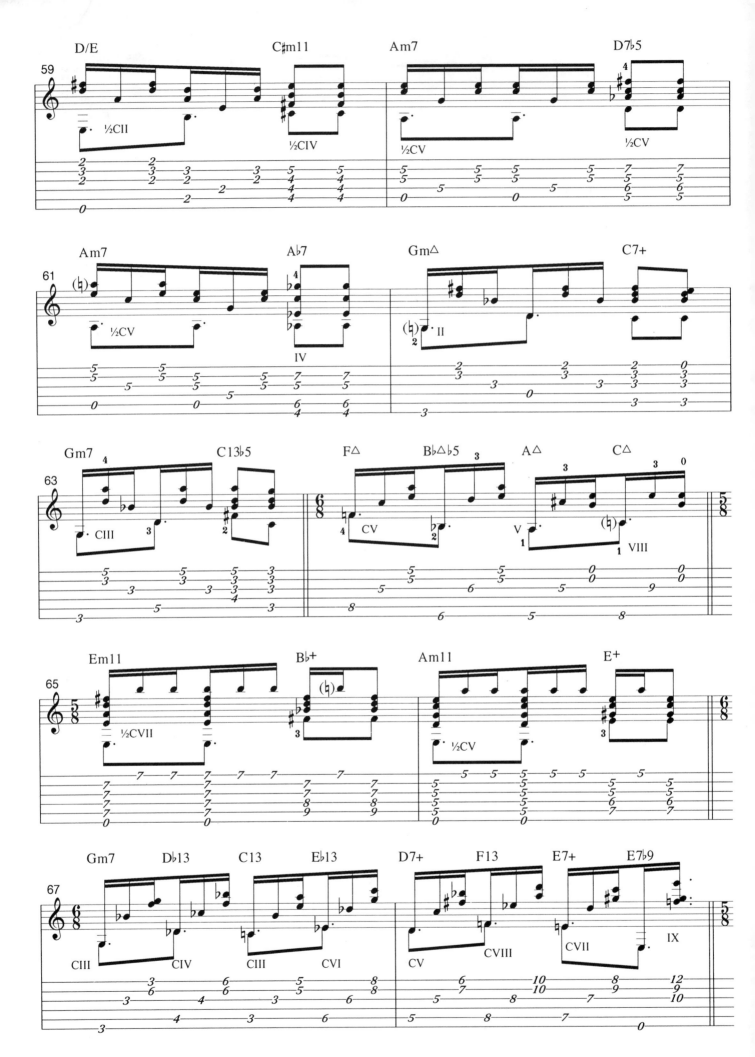

368

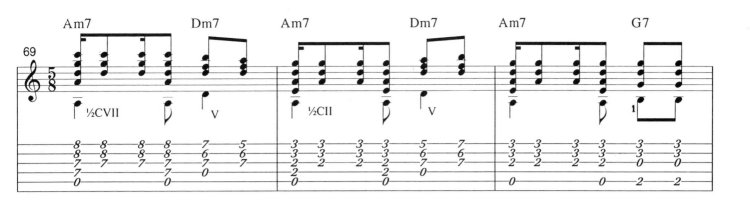

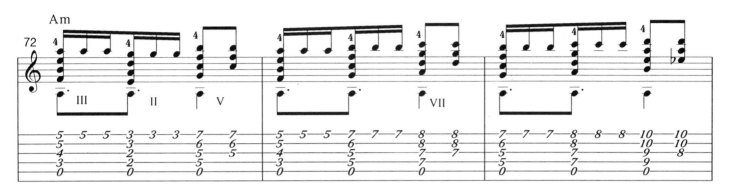

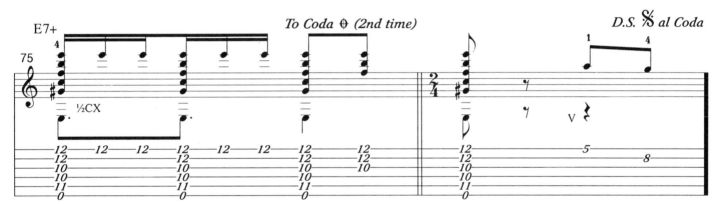

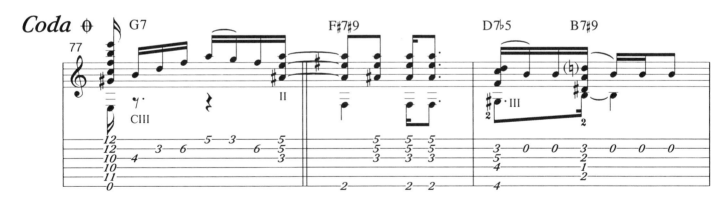

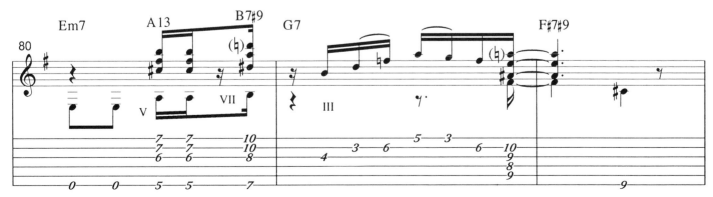

P.39   (P. 160)

P.66   P.322
            P.364
P.72
            P.138
P.138 → P.161 P.153
P.196
            P.99
P.198
            P.150
P.222   P.350
P.264   P.364

P.270

P.276

P.336

GRISWOLD
WORLD
6-27-05
pencil writing
+ dirt JR